2 JOHN 1:7

"Dear children, this is the last hour; and as you have heard that the antichrist is coming, even now many antichrists have come. This is how we know it is the last hour."

The Last Hour

THE LAST HOUR

Sanjay Malwe

Published by Qurate Books Pvt Ltd.

First Published in 2023

ISBN: 9789394600485

Qurate Books Pvt. Ltd.
www.quratebooks.com
Email: info@quratebooks.com

Cover Designed by: Vandana Giby
desiznlab3@gmail.com

INDEX

CHAPTER 1

ANTICIPATING THE RETURN OF JESUS

"When will Jesus' return mummy?" little Suzan asked her mother. Her mother pursed her lips and after throwing her arms in the air replied, "I'm not sure, but I hope Jesus returns soon."

This question has perplexed the Church from the very beginning. Every time the Church has come under pressure, the longing for the return of Jesus has increased. Every Christian looks forward for the era when there will no longer be any pain, and a time when God will wipe away every tear.

The Jews have also been looking in anticipation of their Messiah. They read from the prophecies of Isaiah that the Messiah would bring world peace and he would rule from Zion. They would once again enjoy the privilege of being called God's favorite people. Their enemies would be destroyed and the era of the Messiah would be more glorious than the reign of king David and even Solomon.

The disciples of Jesus recognized him as the Messiah. They were initially shocked when Jesus told them that he would offer his life as a sacrifice. They were troubled by this reality and wanted to know when Jesus would return. They also anticipated that his return would bring about the end of this age, and usher in the kingdom of God.

A few days before Jesus was to give His life for the sins of the world on the cross, He had visited the Jewish temple along with the disciples. The temple was beautiful and the renovation which had begun by king Herod in 20 B.C. had continued for 46 years.

The temple was the center of Jewish life. It was not only the focus of religious ritual but also the place where the holy scriptures were kept.

The disciples like all of Israel were naturally proud of the temple and marveled at its beauty. Imagine their surprise when Jesus told them that the temple would be destroyed.

JESUS PREDICTS THE DESTRUCTION OF THE TEMPLE
MATTHEW 24:1-3

Jesus left the temple area and was going on His way when His disciples came up to point out the temple buildings to Him. 2 But He responded and said to them, "Do you not see all these things? Truly I say to you, not one stone here will be left upon another, which will not be torn down."

3 And as He was sitting on the Mount of Olives, the disciples came to Him privately, saying, "Tell us, when will these things happen, and what will be the sign of Your coming, and of the end of the age?"

The questions of the disciples were two-fold.

1. When will the Temple be destroyed?
2. What will be the signs of the end of the age and the return of Jesus

Jesus began to explain to them the course of events that would unfold from then, on to the end of the age. He began by identifying the signs that the disciples need to be alert about.

WHEN WOULD THE TEMPLE BE DESTROYED?
LUKE 21:5-7

And while some were talking about the temple, that it was adorned with beautiful stones and votive gifts, He said, "As for these things which you are looking at, the days will come in which there will not be left one stone upon another which will not be torn down."

They questioned Him, saying, "Teacher, when therefore will these things happen? And what will be the sign when these things are about to take place?"

THE EVENTS THAT WILL FOLLOW FOR ISRAEL AND THE TEMPLE

LUKE 21:20-24

"But when you see Jerusalem surrounded by armies, then recognize that her desolation is near. Then those who are in Judea must flee to the mountains, and those who are in the midst of the city must leave, and those who are in the country must not enter the city; because these are days of vengeance, so that all things which are written will be fulfilled. Woe to those who are pregnant and to those who are nursing babies in those days; for there will be great distress upon the land and wrath to this people; and they will fall by the edge of the sword, and will be led captive into all the nations; and Jerusalem will be trampled underfoot by the Gentiles until the times of the Gentiles are fulfilled.

With their rejection of the Messiah, Jesus had rightly predicted that Jerusalem and the nation of Israel would be left desolate. Jesus also warned that the Temple would be torn down and not one stone would be left upon another.

In A.D 70, the Romans under the general Titus besieged the city of Jerusalem and a prolonged battle began for the city of Jerusalem. Over a million Jews were killed and over a million Jews were sold as slaves. The temple was torn down and not one stone remained upon another. Jerusalem was left desolate. Eventually they were banned from entering Jerusalem in 135 A.D, and the region of Israel was renamed as "Syria Palestina" in an attempt to minimize Jewish identification with the land of Israel.

Jerusalem has been trampled underfoot by Gentile nations for almost 1900 years.

This was the "Times of the Gentiles".

In 1948 the Jews got back their nation after miraculously defeating the Arab nations who tried to destroy them. Jerusalem however remained in Arab hands until the war of 1967, when the Israel army defeated the Arab nations that had tried once again to destroy them. The place where the Temple had been constructed is now occupied by a Mosque and is under the guardianship of the Jordanian authorities.

The Bible mentions two "Times".

One is "The Time of the Gentiles" and the "Time of the End".

The time of the Gentiles ended in 1967, when Jerusalem came under Israel's rule after a gap of 2000 years. We are now at the period of time which the Bible calls "The Time of the End."

Jesus gave His disciples specific signs that would indicate the spiritual, social and natural climate that be prevalent, even as this age draws to a close.

SIGNS IN THE WORLD

1. Wars and kingdoms against kingdoms (Matthew 24:6-7)
2. Famines and earthquakes (Matthew 13:8)
3. Plagues (Luke 21:11)

SIGNS IN THE CHURCH

1. Deception
2. Persecution
3. A falling away and betrayal
4. False prophets will mislead many
5. The love of many will go cold due to lawlessness

6. The Gospel will be preached as a testimony to the nations

All these signs have been happening with increasing intensity as the coming of Jesus draws near. Remember Jesus said that these signs would be like the birth pangs that a woman in labor experiences. As the birth of the child draws near, the birth pangs will intensify.

Although it is not easy to get a time- line from these signs, we do have the nation of Israel as a prophetic time clock by which we can know the season we live in.

CHAPTER 2

THE ROLE OF ISRAEL IN THE LAST DAYS

The nation of Israel is an enigma in many ways. The Jews are reestablished in the land of their forefathers after almost 2000 years. Such an event has never occurred, where an ethnic community which was exiled from their own land have returned back to their land after so many years.

MOSES AND THE COVENANT

God brought the Israelites out of Egypt where they were slaves, and revealed Himself to them in dramatic ways. The people walked through the Red Sea, ate manna on a daily basis for 40 years, and drank water from a rock. They saw the glory of God on mount Sinai and even heard the audible voice of God.

God promised to give them the land that He had promised to Abraham, Isaac and Jacob. He gave them astounding promises that they would experience if they obeyed His commands. He also warned them of dire consequences if they disobeyed His commands. After God established the Law which was to govern the Israelites, He made a Covenant with the people.

God who is all knowing, knew that the Israelites would break the Covenant that He made with them. In Deuteronomy Chapter 28, Moses gives a prophetic summary of the future of the Israelites. Even before they entered the land promised to them, Moses prophesied that the Israelites would break the Covenant that they had made with God, and would be exiled from their land.

But God also promised to restore them back to the land, once He had dealt with their unfaithfulness.

JOSHUA, JUDGES AND KINGS

The Israelites occupied the Promised land under the leadership of Joshua. The land was then divided into portions for all the tribes of Israel. They then went into a loop of disobedience, defeat by their enemies, repentance and deliverance through a Judge raised by God, for nearly 500 years. The last judge was the prophet, Samuel.

The next phase that Israel went through was the rule of kings. The best of the kings was king David and his son Solomon. Under Solomon, they reached the zenith of their glory and the boundaries of the nation was at its peak. But the seeds of failure were also sown in the reign of Solomon. God allowed the nation to be broken up into two parts; ten tribes which was the Northern nation of Israel and the two tribes in the south which became the nation of Judea.

The Northern kingdom of Israel were led by ungodly kings who took the nation away from God. Although God sent many prophets to warn the nation, it continued on a downward spiral. Eventually they were defeated by the Assyrian kingdom, who not only decimated the nation but also exiled the ten tribes from their land in 722 B.C.

The Southern kingdom of Judea had mixed success. There were some good kings but also some terrible rulers. Ultimately the nation also went into exile in Babylon when they were conquered by the Babylonians in three stages. Jerusalem was razed to the ground and the Jewish Temple was destroyed in 586 B.C.

RESTORATION AND REBUILDING

As prophesied by Jeremiah, the Jews returned to Jerusalem seventy years later. The Babylonians were now replaced by the Medo- Persians and king Cyrus allowed them to return, and rebuild their city. Slowly and steadily, the city and the Temple was rebuilt, but never regained its former glory. Although many Jews returned to their land, a substantial number remained back in Babylon, and the other nations where they had been exiled.

The Medo- Persians were replaced by the Greeks and then the Romans. The Jews only regained control of their land for a brief period during the Greek rule. The Romans controlled the land until the 7th Century A.D.

REJECTION OF THE MESSIAH AND DESOLATION

Starting with Moses, many prophets spoke about the coming Messiah. Their spoke about the glorious times that the nation would experience at the coming of their Messiah. They looked ahead to the time when all their enemies would be defeated and they would be the envy of all the other nations.

But prophets like Isaiah also wrote about the suffering servant who would come to pay the price for the sins of the nation. The Jews could not accept a Messiah who would come as an ordinary human without the outer strapping of power and glory.

When Jesus the Messiah came to redeem mankind, the rulers of Jews rejected Him and even demanded that he be killed. Jesus died on the cross as a sacrifice for the sins of all of us. But the Jewish nation which rejected Jesus, was to pay a huge cost even as they failed to recognize the Messiah. Jesus wept over the city as He prophesied that the city and the Temple would be destroyed, as the Jews failed to recognize the time that the Son of God had visited his people.

MATTHEW 23:37-39

Jerusalem, Jerusalem, who kills the prophets and stones those who have been sent to her! How often I wanted to gather your children together, the way a hen gathers her chicks under her wings, and you were unwilling.

*38 Behold, your house is being left to you desolate! 39 For I say to you, from now on you will not see Me until you say, '**BLESSED IS THE ONE WHO COMES IN THE NAME OF THE LORD!"***

Jerusalem was left desolate in 70 A.D, when the Roman general Titus destroyed Jerusalem and brought down the Temple. Over a million Jews were killed and an equal number sold as slaves.

The Jews continued to resist the Romans until 135 A.D, when they were forbidden from entering Jerusalem and the entire land mass of Israel was renamed Palestina.

JERUSALEM UNDER ISLAMIC CONTROL

After the bitter battles they had endured with the Persians, in which hundreds of lives were lost, the Christians of Jerusalem felt that they had earned possession of the holy city with their life's blood. But less than ten years after the battles between Byzantium and Persia at last came to an end, Caliph Umar's armies arrived at the gates of Jerusalem. They had already subjugated much of the country, and victory over the holy city therefore seemed assured.

When at last the Greek Orthodox Patriarch Sophronius of Jerusalem was forced to surrender in 638 A.D., Umar is believed to have traveled to Jerusalem personally in order to receive the surrender. Umar had become the second Caliph following the death of Abu Bakr, making him one of the earliest successors of Mohammed himself.

But the Caliph was most curious to see the Temple of Solomon, of fabled magnificence. He was horrified to discover that the Temple was in ruins, and the Temple Mount itself had become a rubbish heap in which the city garbage was regularly dumped.

BUILDING ON THE TEMPLE MOUNT

It was at this moment that Temple Mount's identity as a site holy to Islam began to take shape. Umar commanded his men to clear the rubbish from the platform. He then had a rough-hewn wooden mosque built at the southern end of the platform, the first incarnation of what is known today as Al Aqsa.

The Temple Mount was at that time the logical place for a mosque: It had been the site of the Jews' holy Temple, which the Muslims revered, and was not sacred to Christianity. The repercussions of Umar's decision to build a mosque on the holiest site to Judaism would not yet be felt in his lifetime, nor for many years to come.

The Muslims continued to control the entire land of Israel until 1917, when the Ottoman Empire was defeated in the 1st world war. Other than a brief period during the Crusades of the 11th and 12th Century when the Christian crusaders held Jerusalem, Jerusalem has been under the dominion of the Muslim empires under the banner of Islam.

PERSECUTION AND TERROR FOR THE JEWS IN EXILE

The Jews who had scattered to many nations faced death and horror in most of the nations that they had taken refuge. The Spanish inquisition that lasted for more than 300 years was a terrible time for the Jews. Thousands were killed and their wealth confiscated during these dark years. Persecution of the Jews continued in England, France and Germany.

Anti- Semitism reached its height under Hitler who vent his hatred for the Jews. In some of the most brutal acts of human history, over six million Jews were systematically tortured and killed with inhuman brutality. This shook the Jews to the core and they realized that the only place where they would be safe was in the land of their forefathers.

RESTORATION AND REESTABLISHMENT OF THE NATION

Throughout these 2,000 years, Jews, regardless of their current country of residence, continued to view a return to their ancient homeland as an essential part of their identity and a source of hope.

The prophets of God had clearly outlined that the Israelites would be restored to their land. The prophet Ezekiel goes into great detail of how the Lord would restore them. God promised to bring them back from the nations that they were scattered because they had completely violated the Covenant that he had made with Israel. The reason for their restoration was not for the sake of the Israelites, but because they had profaned God's name among the nations they had been exiled.

EZEKIEL 36:22-24

22 "Therefore say to the Israelites, 'This is what the Sovereign LORD says: It is not for your sake, people of Israel, that I am going to do these things, but for the sake of my holy name, which you have profaned among the nations
where you have gone. 23 I will show the holiness of my great name, which has been profaned among the nations, the name you have profaned among them. Then the nations will know that I am the LORD, declares the Sovereign
LORD, when I am proved holy through you before their eyes.24 "'For I will take you out of the nations; I will gather you from all the countries and bring you back into your own land.

The Lord promised to bring the people back to their land and bless the land once they returned. God promised to cause the cities to be inhabited and the waste places to be rebuilt. The desolate land would be cultivated and the nations would marvel at the beauty of the land. Ezekiel writes that the land would resemble the garden of Eden, and the nations of the earth would know that the God of Israel has blessed Israel.

The restoration of Israel would happen in two phases.

First, they would be restored to their land, and then to their God.

The Jews now been restored to their land exactly as the prophets of God declared. Their return to the land has not happened without challenges. The Jewish nation was reborn in 1948. Barely a day old, the nation was plunged into war started by their Arab neighbors who whose goal was to destroy the Jews. Vastly outnumbered in both weapons and numbers they prevailed against their enemies.

The pressure has continued when three of their neighbors sought to attack them in 1967 in what is called the six-day war. Miraculously in just six days, they defeated the armies of three nations namely Egypt, Jordan and Syria.

This war resulted in Jerusalem coming under the control of the Jews for the first time in two thousand years. Jerusalem had been trampled by the Gentile nations for thousands of years. The heart of the Jewish nation, the city of Jerusalem, is firmly with the Jewish people.

However, the place where the Jewish Temple was built has been taken over and a Mosque has replaced the Temple. This mosque was built in 688 A.D called the Dome of the Rock and continues to occupy the spot where the Jewish Temple earlier occupied. The mosque is under the guardianship of the Jordanian authorities.

In spite of being under severe threats continuously from the day of its rebirth, the nation has not only prospered, but is considered among the leading countries in technology, medical breakthroughs and agriculture. Although nearly sixty percent of the land mass is desert, Israel is one of the leading exporters of fruits and vegetables. Truly the hills of Israel have blossomed exactly as the prophet Ezekiel spoke of this day nearly 2500 years ago.

EZEKIEL 36:8-11

But you, mountains of Israel, will produce branches and fruit for my people
Israel, for they will soon come home. [9] *I am concerned for you and will look*
on you with favor; you will be plowed and sown, [10] *and I will cause many*
people to live on you—yes, all of Israel. The towns will be inhabited and the
ruins rebuilt. [11] *I will increase the number of people and animals living on*
you, and they will be fruitful and become numerous. I will settle people on
you as in the past and will make you prosper more than before. Then you
will know that I am the LORD.

WHAT DOES THE FUTURE HOLD FOR THE NATION OF ISRAEL

Although Israel has succeeded in establishing diplomatic relations with some of its neighbors, the Bible warns that there is still trouble ahead. The issue of Jerusalem and the Temple are thorny issues that continue to dominate the mind of the Arabs and the Jews. The Jews have always considered Jerusalem as their most important city from the days of king David. They have a three-thousand-year history with this precious city.

The Arabs under the banner of Islam had conquered Jerusalem in the 7th Century had control over this land for almost a thousand years and they intend to take control once again. The Islamic theology of the end times has convinced them that Jerusalem has to be taken back from the Jews at any cost. The Mosque at the Jewish holy site is called Al Aqsa and is considered the third most holy site for the Muslims. They believe that the prophet of Islam was taken to heaven from this exact Mosque.

Although the nation of Israel has been constantly at war with its much larger neighbors, they have not only managed to increase their territorial land area, but also become a very rich nation.

The prophets have predicted troublesome times for the Jewish nation. Israel would not only be troubled by its neighbors but also be expected to give many concessions to its enemies and even be asked to divide the land; the land that God has promised to the Jewish nation.

ZECHARIAH 12

The burden of the word of the LORD concerning Israel.

Thus declares the LORD who stretches out the heavens, lays the foundation of the earth, and forms the spirit of man within him, 2 "Behold, I am going to make Jerusalem a cup that causes reeling to all the peoples around; and when the siege is against Jerusalem, it will also be against Judah. 3 It will come about in that day that I will make Jerusalem a heavy stone for all the peoples; all who lift it will be severely injured. And all the nations of the earth will be gathered against it.

THE NEAR FUTURE "GOG AND MAGOG" WAR

The prophet Ezekiel has made some clear and very specific prophesies regarding the rebirth of the nation of Israel. He prophesied that Israel would be reborn under the most impossible of situations. That God would bring them out of exile from all the nations and settle them in their own land. He prophesied that the land would flourish with all kinds of harvests and livestock.

Ezekiel also prophesied that the nation would have to face a great danger from a group of nations. More than 2,600 years ago, the prophet Ezekiel warned of a future time when a vast coalition of nations will attack Israel. The leader of this coalition is a man known as Gog, the ruler of Magog ***(Ezekiel 38:1).***

This is why the invading force is known as the Gog of Magog coalition. According to Ezekiel this alliance will send an overwhelming force to invade Israel in the last days. And while the whole world watches, God Himself will destroy the invaders ***(Ezekiel 38:18-23).***

Today for the first time in human history, we see this alliance forming.

THE INVADING NATIONS

Ezekiel identifies these nations as "Magog, Rosh, Meschech, Tubal, Persia, Cush, Put, Gomer, and Beth-togarmah" ***(Ezekiel 38:1-6).***

While the names of these nations have changed over the years, we can still locate them on a map. Below is a list of each nation, followed by its modern-day name:

- **Rosh** = Russia
- **Magog** = Kazakhstan, Uzbekistan, Turkmenistan, Kyrgyzstan, Tajikistan, and Afghanistan
- **Persia** = Iran
- **Cush** = Sudan

- **Put** = Libya
- **Meshech, Tubal, Gomer, and Beth-togarmah** = Turkey

It's been centuries since Ezekiel first recorded these prophecies. Yet, this alliance has never existed. And it certainly hasn't invaded Israel.

Today, we see this alliance coming together.

A DEVELOPING ALLIANCE

Until recently, the nations of Russia and Persia had never formed an alliance of any sort. Economic and military cooperation between Persia (Iran) and Rosh (Russia) had never taken place. But around 1989, this started to change. Today, Iran and Russia are strong allies.

The ongoing civil war in Syria is another area of cooperation between the two countries.

Russia has a vested interest in retaining access to the Syrian naval base in Tartus and stopping the spread of ISIS. As a longtime ally of Syrian President Bashar Assad, Iran also has military forces in Syria. Iran is also the primary sponsor of Hezbollah, a radical terrorist organization. Hezbollah has openly operated in Syria under Assad. So, Russia and Iran share a common interest when it comes to keeping Assad in power.

Because of their common interests, it's easy to see why this alliance will eventually attack Israel. Russian leader Vladimir Putin is determined to restore the former glory of the Soviet Union. But NATO blocks his expansion to the west, and China blocks his expansion to the east. However, Putin could move south and take all the oil wealth of the Middle East.

Only one thing stops him - Israel.

It's clear why Russia wants to eliminate Israel. What about the other nations? It's easy to see why they'll join an invasion force. Religious ideology alone is reason enough. Iran and the other Muslim nations in the Gog of Magog alliance are committed to the total destruction of Israel.

Turkish forces are involved in the ongoing conflict in Syria. Turkey supports forces fighting against the Russian and Iranian backed Syrian government. Yet, the Bible says these three nations will be the principal players in an invasion of Israel.

What might bring them together?

WHEN WILL ALL THIS HAPPEN?

When will this invasion take place? The Bible says it will come "in the latter days" ***(Ezekiel 38:8).*** The original Hebrew word in this verse is "acharith" which means "after-part, latter part, last, close, or end." In other words, this alliance will form in the last days just prior to the return of Jesus Christ. Ezekiel uses this same word "acharith" eight verses later, when he says the invasion will come "in the last days" ***(Ezekiel 38:16).***

This is confirmed again when Ezekiel reveals the Russian leader's thoughts. Gog says to himself, "I will attack the once abandoned cities now populated with the Jews who returned from exile among the nations" ***(Ezekiel 38:12).*** This tells us Russia and its allies will attack the land when it's filled with ***the exiles who return from among the nations***. The target can only be modern day Israel.

This means the invasion is coming in our day and time.

Ezekiel stresses this fact again and again when he says the invasion will occur "after Israel's people have been gathered from among many nations" ***(Ezekiel 38:8)*** and "when I bring my people home from among the enemy nations" ***(Ezekiel 39:27).*** This return home from among many nations has happened only once in all of human history - modern day Israel.

EZEKIEL 38:8

After many days you will be summoned; in the latter years you will come into the land that is restored from the sword, whose inhabitants have been gathered from many nations to the mountains of Israel which had been a continual waste; but its people were brought out from the nations, and they are living securely, all of them.

IS THIS BATTLE THE SAME AS THE BATTLE OF ARMAGEDDON?

Bible teachers differ on this battle. There are similarities in both the battle of Ezekiel as well as the battle described by John in Revelation 16.

- In both battles, vast armies want to destroy Israel.
- The Lord intervenes and saves Israel in both battles.
- The birds of the air are called for a feast made up of the bodies of mighty men of war and of horses. (Ezekiel 39:17-20), (Revelation 19:17-18)

Some teachers believe that they are two different battles. The "Gog and Magog" war as it is called in the book of Ezekiel happens before the battle of Armageddon. Since the weapons used by the invading armies are used by Israel as fuel for seven years, it is assumed that this battle will happen at least seven years before the battle of Armageddon. (Ezekiel 39:9)

THE GREAT TRIBULATION

We first read about the time of great tribulation in the book of Daniel. The prophet Daniel wrote about a season of such terror that will come upon the nation, that Israel that it will be unparalleled.

The terror will be of such a magnitude, that no nation has ever witnessed such trouble in the past or will ever occur again.

DANIEL 12:1-4

Now at that time Michael, the great prince who stands guard over the sons of your people, will arise. And there will be a time of distress such as never occurred since there was a nation until that time; and at that time your people, everyone who is found written in the book, will be rescued.

[2] And many of those who sleep in the dust of the ground will awake, these to everlasting life, but the others to disgrace and everlasting contempt. [3] And those who have insight will shine like the glow of the expanse of heaven, and those who lead the many to righteousness, like the stars forever and ever.

[4] But as for you, Daniel, keep these words secret and seal up the book until the end of time; many will roam about, and knowledge will increase."

The Nation of Israel has witnessed many horrors in its history. They were defeated by the Assyrians, the Babylonians, the Medo-Persians, the Greeks and the Romans. The Romans crushed them so severely, that they were unable to take root in their land for almost 2000 years.

The Jews faced persecution in almost every nation that they were in exile. The most damage however was done to them under Hitler who masterminded the death of six million Jews.

The Israelites are back in their land after many years. They continue not only to survive, but thrive under extreme pressure from their neighbors, who have theological reasons to exterminate the Jewish nation.

Yet the Bible states that there are greater horrors ahead. The time of the great tribulation will be just before the return of Jesus. The prophecy of the prophet Daniel clearly points out that this time of terror will be just prior to the resurrection from the dead. (Daniel 12:2-3)

JESUS ALSO SPOKE ABOUT THE GREAT TRIBULATION

When Jesus spoke about the end of the age, He referred to the prophecy of Daniel. Jesus warned the nation of Israel that they would encounter a time of great tribulation. This time of terror would be so severe that no nation has ever encountered so much trouble in the past, nor will any nation experience such trouble after that time.

MATTHEW 24:15-22

Therefore, when you see the ABOMINATION OF DESOLATION which was spoken of through Daniel the prophet, standing in the holy place—let

the reader understand— [16] then those who are in Judea must flee to the
mountains. [17] Whoever is on the housetop must not go down to get things
out of his house. [18] And whoever is in the field must not turn back to get his
cloak. [19] But woe to those women who are pregnant, and to those who are
nursing babies in those days! [20] Moreover, pray that when you flee, it will not
be in the winter, or on a Sabbath.

[21] For then there will be a great tribulation, such as has not occurred since
the beginning of the world until now, nor ever will again. [22] And if those days
had not been cut short, no life would have been saved; but for the sake of the
elect those days will be cut short.

When would this time of tribulation occur?

Jesus said that it would occur joust prior to His return.

There are two events which will take place immediately after the great tribulation.

The return of Jesus coming in a cloud with power and great glory.

The gathering of the elect by the angels.

MATTHEW 24:29-31

[29] "But immediately after the tribulation of those days THE SUN WILL
BE DARKENED, AND THE MOON WILL NOT GIVE ITS LIGHT, AND
THE STARS WILL FALL *from the sky, and the powers of the heavens will*
be shaken. [30] And then the sign of the Son of Man will appear in the sky, and
then all the tribes of the earth will mourn, and they will see the SON OF
MAN COMING ON THE CLOUDS OF THE SKY *with power and great*
glory.

[31] And He will send forth His angels with A GREAT TRUMPET BLAST, *and*
THEY WILL GATHER TOGETHER *His elect from the four winds, from*
one end of the sky to the other.

It important to keep our focus on Israel. Israel is the clock by which we are able to know the end times. God has chosen Israel to be a sign for the nations. For almost two thousand years the people of Israel were in exile. The clock had stopped ticking. Now the people of Israel are back in the land of their forefathers. The clock has begun to tick once again.

Every prophecy regarding their exile as well as the rebirth of the nation has come to pass exactly as prophesied by the prophets of God. When Jesus prophesied about the time of the tribulation and the "Abomination of Desolation" he spoke specifically about the nation of Judea and warned the people to flee from the land when they see this prophecy fulfilled.

God has never forgotten His people. Although they lost their way and went into exile, God has His eye upon the nation. He has restored his people and blessed them.

They are a sign for the Nations.

JEREMIAH 31:35-37

35 *This is what the LORD says,*
He who gives the sun for light by day
And the fixed order of the moon and the stars for light by night,
Who stirs up the sea so that its waves roar—
The LORD of armies is His name:
36 *"If this fixed order departs from Me," declares the LORD,*
"Then the descendants of Israel also will cease to be a nation before Me forever."
37 *This is what the LORD says:*
"If the heavens above can be measured
And the foundations of the earth searched out below,
Then I will also reject all the descendants of Israel
For everything that they have done," declares the LORD.

CHAPTER 3

MANY ANTICHRISTS AND "THE ANTICHRIST"

Is the Antichrist alive today? He could be. Will we recognize him?

Any mention of the Antichrist sets off feelings of discomfort in any Christian, who takes the Bible seriously. Images of terror and forced worship immediately spring up.

The Antichrist is the opposite of Christ. Just as Christ came to earth to do the Father's will; the Antichrist will come to do the will of Satan. He will be Satan manifest in the form of man.

The Greek word used here for "Antichrist" can have two meanings. First, it can mean "against Christ," in the sense of someone or some power who opposes Christ and His work. Second, the word can mean "instead of Christ," signifying a person or power who takes the place of Christ—a counterfeit Christ.

Satan's whole ambition is to be like God in power and might, and he works for this with all of his might, night and day. His intention is to replace God, and he will send the Antichrist as a means to do this. The Antichrist will proclaim himself as God, and assert himself as ruler of this world. But what kind of a world would be willing to accept the emissary of Satan as Lord? Is it possible that this world we live in now has come to such a state?

THE SPIRIT OF ANTICHRIST

The prevailing spirit in the world is the spirit of Antichrist, which has been working since the earliest days of the Church. The spirit of Antichrist can be summed up as every spirit that does not confess that Jesus Christ has come in the flesh.

1 JOHN 4:1-3

Beloved, do not believe every spirit, but test the spirits to see whether they are from God, because many false prophets have gone out into the world. By this you know the Spirit of God: every spirit that confesses that Jesus Christ has come in the flesh is from God; and every spirit that does not confess Jesus is not from God; this is the spirit of the antichrist, of which you have heard that it is coming, and now it is already in the world.

2 JOHN 1:7

"For many deceivers have gone out into the world who do not confess Jesus Christ as coming in the flesh. This is a deceiver and an antichrist"

According to God's Word, these antichrists in the early church were counterfeit Christians who had split away from the body of true believers. They were deceivers who had not really experienced a genuine gospel conversion. They were liars who denied that Jesus was the promised Messiah.

DENYING THE "FATHER AND THE SON"

1 JOHN 2:22,

"Who is a liar but he who denies that Jesus is the Christ?
He is antichrist who denies the Father and the Son."

The Bible declares that Jesus is the Son of God who came to earth as the "Son of Man" – fully God and fully human. He was born in human likeness and paid the price for the sins of all mankind. Now he is seated at the right hand of the Father and is worshipped by the hosts of heaven. The spirit of Antichrist denies the relationship between the Father and His son Jesus. It attacks the reality of the death and resurrection of Jesus.

There are many religions practiced all over the earth, each with its unique philosophies. But no religion speaks against the revelation, that Jesus Christ is the Son of God. There is however one ideology which stands directly in conflict with the most fundamental truth of the Bible?

It is the religion of Islam.

Islam accepts the virgin birth of Jesus and He is held in high regard by the Muslims. He is acknowledged as a prophet and a wise teacher. It records that Jesus was a miracle worker and that He ascended to heaven.

But the most fundamental truth that Jesus declared about himself is what Islam denies. The fact that Jesus is the "Son of God. It also denies that Jesus died on the cross or rose again from the dead. Even the name of Jesus is renamed as Isa.

The reality is that the Isa of the Quran is not the Jesus of the Bible.

THE FOUNDATIONS OF THE SPIRIT OF THE ANTICHRIST

1. It denies that Jesus is the Messiah
2. It denies that Jesus is the "Son of God"

WAS THE EARLY CHURCH EXPECTING THE ANTI-CHRIST?

1 JOHN 2:18

"Dear children, this is the last hour; and as you have heard that the antichrist is coming, even now many antichrists have come. This is how we know it is the last hour."

In this verse, God is speaking to the early Christian church. Obviously, the word "hour" is used in a figurative sense. The same Greek word is often translated as "time;" in fact, that is how the King James Version of the Bible translates it in this same verse. God is stating that humanity is living in the last time, the last era, and the last period of earth's history.

God is reminding the early church believers of a prophecy they had already heard—namely, that the Antichrist was going to come. (There were many other antichrists already in existence during the era of the early church) The spirit of Antichrist was already at work from the beginning of church history, and many individuals rose up against Christ as antichrists.

God also says that in addition to the coming of "the" Antichrist—a unique Antichrist would arrive on the scene in the last days just prior to the return of Jesus. The Bible warns us that in the last days, one individual who will personify everything that is against Christ will rise up to persecute the people of God.

The Antichrist will be a world figure who dominates the political landscape of the earth. He will have authority that is given to him by Satan himself. This will be Satan's final attempt to overthrow the rule of God Almighty in this age. It will be the last throw of the dice before his time is up, when Jesus returns to take back control over His creation.

THE TITLES OF THE ANTICHRIST

The Antichrist is not an exclusively New Testament figure. He is first described in the book of Daniel. He is also mentioned by the Apostle John, as well as Paul of the New Testament.

Jesus doesn't mention the Antichrist directly, but gives a reference of the kind of horror that this individual will unleash on the world, with a primary focus on the Jewish nation.

Jesus calls this time of trouble "the great tribulation" and the identification clue is called "the abomination of Desolation"

The titles of the Antichrist include:

1. The "little Horn" Daniel 7
2. The "Man of Sin / Lawlessness 2 Thessalonians 2:3-6

3. The Antichrist	1 John 2:22, 1 John 4:1-3, 2 John1:7
4. The Beast from the Sea	Revelation 13
5. The Beast from the Abyss	Revelation 11:7; 17:8; 19:9
6. The Scarlet Beast	Revelation 17

THE DETAILS OF THE ANTICHRIST

1. He receives his authority from Satan.
2. He recovers from a deadly wound at which the whole world is astonished and follows him.
3. He establishes total control of all nations of the earth.
4. He is assisted by a group of ten kingdoms who forge an alliance with him.(Revelation 17:12-13)
5. He takes control over Jerusalem. (Revelation 11:1-2)
6. He takes control of all the institutions as well all-financial institutions.
7. He demands worship from everyone.
8. He will persecute the people of God and overcome them.
9. He will have authority for a period of 3.5 years
10. He will gather an army to fight against Jesus who returns as the King of Kings. (Rev 19:19)
11. He will be cast into the lake of fire (Revelation 19:20)

REVELATION 13:1-10

And the dragon stood on the sand of the seashore.

Then I saw a beast coming up out of the sea, having ten horns and seven heads, and on his horns were ten crowns, and on his heads were blasphemous names. [2] And the beast that I saw was like a leopard, and his feet were like those of a bear, and his mouth like the mouth of a lion. And the dragon gave him his power and his throne, and great authority. [3] I saw one of his heads as if it had been fatally wounded, and his fatal wound was healed. And the whole earth was amazed and followed after the beast; [4] they worshiped the dragon because he gave his authority to the beast; and they worshiped the beast, saying, "Who is like the beast, and who is able to wage war with him?"
[5] A mouth was given to him speakingarrogant words and blasphemies, and authority to act for forty-two months was given to him. [6] And he opened his mouth in blasphemies against God, to blaspheme His name and His tabernacle, that is, those who dwell in heaven.

[7] It was also given to him to make war with the saints and to overcome them, and authority was given to him over every tribe, people, language, and nation. [8] All who live on the earth will worship him, everyone whose name has not been written since the foundation of the world in the book of life of the Lamb who has been slaughtered. [9] If anyone has an ear, let him hear. [10] If anyone is destined for captivity, to captivity he goes; if anyone kills with the sword, with the sword he must be killed. Here is the perseverance and the faith of the saints.

THE FALSE PROPHET WHO ASSISTS THE ANTICHRIST

The Antichrist will not be alone in this endeavor to deceive mankind. He will receive assistance from another individual whom the Bible calls "The beast from the earth. "This beast has two horns like a lamb but he speaks the language of the Dragon. He will pretend to represent Jesus but will in-fact follow the agenda of Satan. Let's list the details of the false prophet.

1. He exercises all the authority of the Antichrist.
2. He makes the earth and those who dwell in it worship the Antichrist.
3. He performs great signs, even makes fire come down from heaven to the earth.

4. He deceives those who dwell on earth and causes them to make an image of the beast.
5. He gives breath to the image of the beast.
6. Those who refuse to bow down to this image will be killed.
7. He forces men to be given a mark of the beast on their right hand or forehead.
8. He enforces the rule that no one will be able to buy or sell without the mark.

REVELATION 13:11-18

11 Then I saw another beast coming up out of the earth; and he had two
horns like a lamb, and he spoke as a dragon. 12 He exercises all the authority
of the first beast in his presence. And he makes the earth and those who live
on it worship the first beast, whose fatal wound was healed. 13 He performs
great signs, so that he even makes fire come down out of the sky to the earth
in the presence of people. 14 And he deceives those who live on the earth
because of the signs which it was given him to perform in the presence of the
beast, telling those who live on the earth to make an image to the beast who
had the wound of the sword and has come to life.

15 And it was given to him to give breath to the image of the beast, so that
the image of the beast would even speak and cause all who do not worship
the image of the beast to be killed. 16 And he causes all, the small and the
great, the rich and the poor, and the free and the slaves, to be given a mark
on their right hands or on their foreheads, 17 and he decrees that no one will
be able to buy or to sell, except the one who has the mark, either the name
of the beast or the number of his name. 18 Here is wisdom. Let him who has
understanding calculate the number of the beast, for the number is that of a
man; and his number is six hundred and sixty-six.

CHAPTER 4

TRACKING THE ANTICHRIST

The world is a mess and is rapidly descending into a vortex of unbridled immorality as well as turmoil in every sphere of life. The people of the world are currently desperate for a savior who will rescue them from all their self-inflicted problems. The threat of war, economic uncertainty, terrorism, disease, and the seeming meaninglessness of life are all preparing humankind to accept what will be its last great human emperor, which the Bible describes in vivid detail.

Let's unlock the details that are given in the world of God regarding the Antichrist.

The many names of the Antichrist

1. The "little Horn"	Daniel 7
2. The "Man of Sin / Lawlessness	2 Thessalonians 2:1-12
3. The Antichrist	1 John 2:22, 1 John 4:1-3, 2 John 1:7
4. The Beast from the Sea	Revelation 13
5. The Beast from the Abyss	Revelation 11:7; 17:8; 19:9
6. The Scarlet Beast	Revelation 17

1. THE LITTLE HORN

The prophet Daniel writing over two thousand five hundred years ago has a dream in which he literally is given the remaining history of the earth. The images are very vivid and in the language of typologies.

In his dream he sees four beasts that come out of the sea. The sea in question is the Mediterranean Sea. Each beast looks different from the other. The prophet then receives the meaning of the dream and he writes it down. The Beasts are four kingdoms that will arise on the earth one after another. Daniel was writing from Babylon during the reign of the last ruler of Babylon named Belshazzar.

These great beasts, which are four, are four kings, which shall arise out of the earth. **Daniel 7:17**

Looking through history we can identify each kingdom.

The common factor for each of these kingdoms is that they ruled over the nation of Israel. Israel is the clock by which we know the time for the end of this age. Let's take a look at these kingdoms.

BABYLON - THE LION WITH WINGS OF AN EAGLE
DANIEL 7:4

The first was like a lion and had the wings of an eagle. I kept looking until its wings were plucked, and it was lifted up from the ground and made to stand on two feet like a man; a human mind also was given to it.

The Lion of Babylon is an ancient Babylonian symbol. The Lion of Babylon symbolically represented the King of Babylon. The depiction is based on the Mesopotamian lion, which used to roam in the region. The wings being plucked is a reference to the time when God had humbled Nebuchadnezzar. God had caused Nebuchadnezzar to lose his mind, and become like an animal for seven years. He was then restored and given back his kingdom, after which he acknowledged the sovereignty of God. This is recorded in detail in Daniel Chapter 4.

THE BEAR (MEDO – PERSIA)
DANIEL 7:5

And behold, another beast, a second one, resembling a bear. And it was raised up on one side, and three ribs were in its mouth between its teeth; and thus, they said to it, 'Arise, devour much meat!'

The Bear represented the joint kingdom of the Medo – Persians. The Persians were more powerful than the Medes as represented by the raised side. Before the two kingdoms united, Media was the dominant kingdom. But in 550 B.C.E., the Medes came under the control of Persian King Cyrus II, who thereafter ruled over the kingdom of Medo-Persia. Centered in the region north of the Persian Gulf, this vast realm eventually stretched from the Aegean Sea to Egypt to northwestern India and included Judea.

Medo-Persia ruled over the Jewish nation for more than 200 years—from the overthrow of Babylon in 539 B.C. until Medo-Persia itself was defeated by the Greeks in 331 B.C.

THE LEOPARD (GREECE)
DANIEL 7:6

After this I kept looking, and behold, another one, like a leopard, which had on its back four wings of a bird; the beast also had four heads, and dominion was given to it.

The Grecian empire under the dynamic young leader Alexander the Great swept over this entire region. The Leopard is a strong and swift animal. The four wings represented the speed in which Alexander would conquer nation after nation. In a period of just ten years, he had an empire that stretched from Greece to the borders of India. Thereafter, Alexander continued to expand his empire until his premature death in 323 B.C.E., at the age of 32.

The four heads represent the division of the kingdom into four major parts after Alexander.

No single individual succeeded Alexander as absolute ruler, nor did any of his offspring. Rather, his four leading generals—Lysimachus, Cassander, Seleucus, and Ptolemy—"proclaimed themselves kings" and took over the empire.

THE TERRIBLE 4TH BEAST (ROME)
DANIEL 7:7

After this I kept looking in the night visions, and behold, a fourth beast, dreadful and terrifying and extremely strong; and it had large iron teeth. It devoured and crushed and trampled down the remainder with its feet; and it was different from all the beasts that were before it, and it had ten horns.

In 168 B.C., it was the Roman empire's turn to enact its supreme rule upon the region.

Prophetically this terrible looking beast perfectly symbolizes this kingdom: its military strength and discipline, its domination over many conquered nations, its laws imposed on all people far and wide.

The Roman empire was in power during the time of Jesus and continued to rule through its capital Rome till 324 A.D.

Constantinople became the new capital of the Roman empire through Emperor Constantine the Great, after whom it was named, and dedicated on 11 May 330. It is located in Turkey.

The western side of Rome collapsed under the onslaught of the barbarian tribes.

The eastern side of Rome continued as the Byzantine empire until the year 1453 A. D when it was taken over by the Ottoman empire.

It is in this geographical area that comprises Turkey and the Middle-East going right up to India, parts of North Africa and a very small portion of eastern Europe that the Bible draws our attention to. This area is completely dominated by Islam. What is important to note is that Islam is a political religion that demands complete dominance of the world.

THE TEN HORNS AND THE "LITTLE HORN"

The Ten horns represent ten kings who will arise just prior the second coming of Jesus.

But they will be led by an individual whom the Bible calls "The Little Horn"

This Man will oppose God and speak abominations against the "Son of God" – Jesus

DANIEL 7:24

As for the ten horns, out of this kingdom ten kings will arise;

THE "LITTLE HORN" DANIEL 7:24-25

and another will arise after them, and he will be different from the previous ones and will subdue three kings. He will speak out against the Highest and wear down the saints of the Highest One, and he will intend to make alterations in times and in law; and they will be given into his hand for a time, times, and half a time.

DANIEL 7:20-22

.... the other horn which came up, and before which three of them fell, namely, that horn which had eyes and a mouth uttering great boasts and which was larger in appearance than its associates. I kept looking, and that horn was waging war with the saints and overpowering them until the Ancient of Days came and judgment was passed in favor of the saints of the Highest One, and the time arrived when the saints took possession of the kingdom.

Here we are given a spectacular glimpse of the way events will unfold in the future.

We are introduced to this diabolical person called the "little Horn" who not only blasphemes against the living God, but also tries to exalt himself as god and demand worship form everyone.

The "Little Horn leads the "Ten kings". He will be different and unlike the kings before him. He will be a vile man who will not only oppose God but also severely persecute the people of God. He will attempt to make changes in the Law and institute unholy laws. The people of God will be given into his hand for a time called "*a time, times, and half a time.*" This is a period of three and a half years.

During the three and a half years the "Little Horn" who is also referred to as "The Anti-Christ causes great distress to the people of God. He will however have a horrific end. He will be judged and taken away to be cast into the "Lake of fire"

THE KINGDOMS OF THE EARTH HANDED OVER TO THE "SON OF MAN" – JESUS

DANIEL 7:26-27

But the court will sit for judgment, and his dominion will be taken away, annihilated and destroyed forever. Then the sovereignty, the dominion and the greatness of all the kingdoms under the whole heaven will be given to the people of the saints of the Highest One; His kingdom will be an everlasting kingdom, and all the dominions will serve and obey Him.'

While all this is happening however, God is on His throne in Heaven. There is the scene of a courtroom where the books are opened. The "Little Horn" is judged and cast into the lake of fire. In this manner the Antichrist, as well as the false prophet will be judged by the true God. This judgement will take place even as the Messiah returns to set up his millennium kingdom.

The sovereignty, dominion and greatness of all the kingdoms under heaven will be given to the people of the saints of God. Jesus who will have returned in glory along with the angels, is the ruler of this kingdom that is an everlasting kingdom. All nations and people of every language and tongue, will serve and obey Him.

Summarizing everything we have learnt in Daniel chapter seven; it is very evident that the Antichrist who is called "the little horn" in Daniel arrives on the world scene just before the return of Jesus. He is allowed dominion over the people of the earth for a period of three and a half years. Jesus will then return and establish His everlasting kingdom in which the saints of God will reign with Him.

2. THE "MAN OF SIN / LAWLESSNESS

Paul writes about the Antichrist but names him the "Man of Sin". This is a very apt name, for he will be the epistome of everything evil. He will literally be Satan in the flesh. Paul is writing to the Thessalonians that they were not to be troubled by reports that the Lord Jesus has returned and that the gathering together to Him (rapture) has already happened.

Paul then goes on to give the clue to knowing when the return of Jesus will be just round the corner. Immediately prior to the return to Jesus, the "Man of Sin" will reveal himself.

2 THESSALONIANS 2:1-12

Now we ask you, brothers and sisters, regarding the coming of our Lord Jesus
Christ and our gathering together to Him, 2 that you not be quickly shaken
from your composure or be disturbed either by a spirit, or a message, or a
letter as if from us, to the effect that the day of the Lord has come. 3 No one
is to deceive you in any way! For it will not come unless the apostasy comes
first, and the man of lawlessness is revealed, the son of destruction, 4 who
opposes and exalts himself above every so-called god or object of worship, so
that he takes his seat in the temple of God, displaying himself as being God. 5
Do you not remember that while I was still with you, I was telling you these
things? 6 And you know what restrains him now, so that he will be revealed
in his time. 7 For the mystery of lawlessness is already at work; only He who
now restrains will do so until He is removed. 8 Then that lawless one will be
revealed, whom the Lord will eliminate with the breath of His mouth and
bring to an end by the appearance of His coming; 9 that is, the one whose
coming is in accord with the activity of Satan, with all power and false

signs and wonders, [10] and with all the deception of wickedness for those who perish, because they did not accept the love of the truth so as to be saved. [11] For this reason God will send upon them a deluding influence so that they will believe what is false, [12] in order that they all may be judged who did not believe the truth, but took pleasure in wickedness.

What details does Paul present to us regarding the Antichrist?

1. The Antichrist will be revealed just prior to the return of Jesus.
2. He will exalt himself as God and oppose the true God.
3. He takes his seat in the Temple of God (which is in Jerusalem)
4. The Antichrist will come with the authority and power of Satan.
5. He will display signs and wonders and deceive the nations.
6. God will send a deluding influence so that those who have not accepted the truth will believe what is false and accept the antichrist.
7. This will lead to judgement for those who have rejected the love of God.
8. The "man of sin" will be judged by being cast into the lake of fire.
9. This will happen when Jesus returns and gathers his people to Himself.

3. THE ANTICHRIST

The Apostle John names him the "Antichrist".

Among the many names given to this evil entity who will be revealed in the last days, the most famous is the name "Antichrist". This name brings visions of persecutions for the Jews and Christians that are of a scale never seen before. He will be the very embodiment of everything evil and vile. And yet the world which has turned its back to the living God, will accept him as their leader. Not only would they accept him, but also worship him as though he was God.

There have been many agents of Satan throughout the history of mankind. Satan in his rebellion against God, also has at his command one third of the angels who fell with him and who are commonly called demons. Satan brought his rebellion to the earth as he has gone about deceiving mankind to join in his rebellion towards God. The final display of the evil one will be evident through this last ungodly agent called the Antichrist.

As we read the letters written by John, we get information of this agent of Satan.

1 JOHN 2:18-22

Children, it is the last hour; and just as you heard that antichrist is coming,
even now many antichrists have appeared; from this we know that it is
the last hour. [19] *They went out from us, but they were not really of us; for*
if they had been of us, they would have remained with us; but they went
out, so that it would be evident that they all are not of us. [20] *But you have*
an anointing from the Holy One, and you all know. [21] *I have not written to*
you because you do not know the truth, but because you do know it, and
because no lie is of the truth.

[22] *Who is the liar except the one who denies that Jesus is the Christ?*

This is the antichrist, the one who denies the Father and the Son.

1 JOHN 4:1-3

Beloved, do not believe every spirit, but test the spirits to see whether they are from God, because many false prophets have gone out into the world. By this you know the Spirit of God: every spirit that confesses that Jesus Christ has come in the flesh is from God; and every spirit that does not confess Jesus is not from God; this is the spirit of the antichrist, of which you have heard that it is coming, and now it is already in the world.

2 JOHN 1:7

7 For many deceivers have gone out into the world, those who do not acknowledge Jesus Christ as coming in the flesh. This is the deceiver and the antichrist.

THE SUMMARY OF THE SPIRIT OF THE ANTICHRIST

1. It denies that Jesus is the Messiah
2. It denies that Jesus is the "Son of God"

The entire goal of Satan has been to cause mankind to join in his rebellion against God. This has brought about sin and destruction and untold misery on the earth. Jesus the Messiah being the "Son of God" came to us as the "Son of Man" and paid for our rebellion by offering his life on the cross.

The spirit of the Antichrist has worked nonstop from the very beginning to deny that Jesus is the Messiah. This spirit has tried relentlessly to deceive people, so that they would deny Jesus as the Son of God.

4. THE BEAST FROM THE SEA

Perhaps the most information we get about the Antichrist is from the book of Revelation in chapter thirteen. But before we need to dwell on the chapter twelve. This chapter lays the foundation of what is the background to the coming of the Antichrist.

In chapter twelve, we are given the background to the war that is happening in heaven. Satan has rebelled against God along with a third of the angels. His main target has been the nation of Israel. God had revealed that the Messiah would come from the descendant of Abraham. Satan has tried through the centuries to destroy the descendants of Abraham.

He attempted through Pharoah, to destroy the line of the Israelites when they were in Egypt and were made slaves. He used a mad dictator named

Antiochus Epiphanies around 168 B.C to pervert the Jewish nation, by forcing them to worship Greek gods and not only forbade the Jewish customs, but also stopped the Jews from worshipping at their temple.

He attempted to kill the Messiah at his birth through king Herod.

When his attempts failed at stopping the work of Jesus the Messiah, Satan has from then on tried to get rid of the Jews. Satan knows from the scriptures that the Messiah will return to Israel during the last battle called the "battle of Armageddon" to save the Jewish nation from annihilation.

Therefore, Satan's attempt has been threefold.

1. Annihilate the Jews so they cannot return to their nation.
2. Stop them from getting back to the land promised to them.
3. Attempt to destroy people of Israel who are back in the land of their forefathers.

Throughout the last two thousand years, they have been persecuted and literally thrown out of almost every nation that they were in exile.

The most severe of these attempts to destroy them, came from Adolph Hitler in 1933 to 1939 A.D. The Nazi's under Hitler targeted the Jews as being racially inferior. Their properties were seized even as they place of worship were destroyed. The Jews were sent to concentration camps where they were brutally massacred. The total number of Jews killed under Hitler were six million men woman and children.

THE JEWS BACK IN THEIR OWN LAND

Because many of the laws required residency in their ancient homeland, a longing to return to Zion also bonded communities of Jews now living on different sides of the world and without a common language. "Next year in Jerusalem" became the heartfelt motto for Jews no matter their age, ethnicity, place of residency, or language.

The holocaust that the Jewish people experienced, and the terror they went through in some nations pushed them to consider having their own nation. The Jews understood that only in their own land, would they finally find rest.

Slowly but surely, in small numbers initially and then also in mass migration, the Jews came back to their land. Almost half of the Jews of the world live in the Land of Israel today, where they have enjoyed 70 years of statehood and endured 70 years of a constant state of war and thousands of terror attacks.

The attempt to destroy the nation of Israel which has been reestablished, has been well documented. To describe their survival as a miracle is justified and correctly assigns responsibility for it to God, who affirmed several times in the Hebrew Scriptures that the people of Israel would never cease to be a nation before Him (Jeremiah 31:36; Isaiah 66:22). Even if all the other nations are brought to an end, they would remain (Jeremiah 30:11).

The people of Israel had a unique calling; to bless the world with God's redemptive plan—and they would suffer greatly for it. The powers of evil would forever fight against God's plan because it would bring an end to their power on earth. They would attempt to stop it by destroying the people called to bring it about. The God of Israel understood the difficult place that this put His people in, and therefore guaranteed their survival.

Satan has always managed to raise enemies who would try to destroy the Jews. In these last days, the Arabs under the banner of Islam and the excuse of the Palestinian problem have tried time and again to destroy Israel.

Satan's final attempt to destroy Israel will be through his chosen vessel – the Antichrist or in the name shown to us in the book of Revelation called the "Beast from the Sea."

THE KINGDOM OF THE ANTICHRIST

Can we know the location that the Antichrist rules and the extent of his kingdom. The Bible gives us some clues to the area where this evil world leader will rule. We however need to read the book of Daniel also. Daniel the prophet records a dream that he receives in chapter seven. He sees four beasts that arise out of the sea. Each beast is a symbol for a nation that had ruled over the nation of Israel.

The first beast is a lion which was a symbol of the Babylon empire.

The second beast is a bear which was a symbol of the Medo-Persian empire.

The third beast is a leopard which had four heads which was the symbol of the Grecian empire.

The fourth beast is a terrible looking beast with ten horns.

The book of Revelation chapter thirteen, gives the description of the "Beast from the Sea" who looks like a bear, has a mouth as a lion and the feet of a bear. It has seven heads. It also has ten horns.

How do we decipher this revelation?

The answer is that the kingdom of the Antichrist will be a combination of the empires of Medo- Persia, Babylon, Greece and Rome. We must keep in mind that the Roman empire split into two parts; the Western and the Eastern part. The Eastern part which whose capital was Constantinople (now Istanbul in Turkey) was renamed as the Byzantine empire lasted almost a thousand years after the western part had collapsed.

The seven heads correspond to the empires of Babylon, Medo- Persia, Rome and Greece.

(Greece broke up into four parts after the sudden death of Alexander the Great)

The ten horns are the ten kings who will join hands with the "Beast from the Sea" in the last days before the return of Jesus.

The headquarters of the Antichrist will be Jerusalem. He will sit in the place where the Jewish temple was, and demand worship from all mankind. Jesus describes this period as the great tribulation and the final sign will be "The abomination that causes desolation"

THE KINGDOM OF THE ANTICHRIST

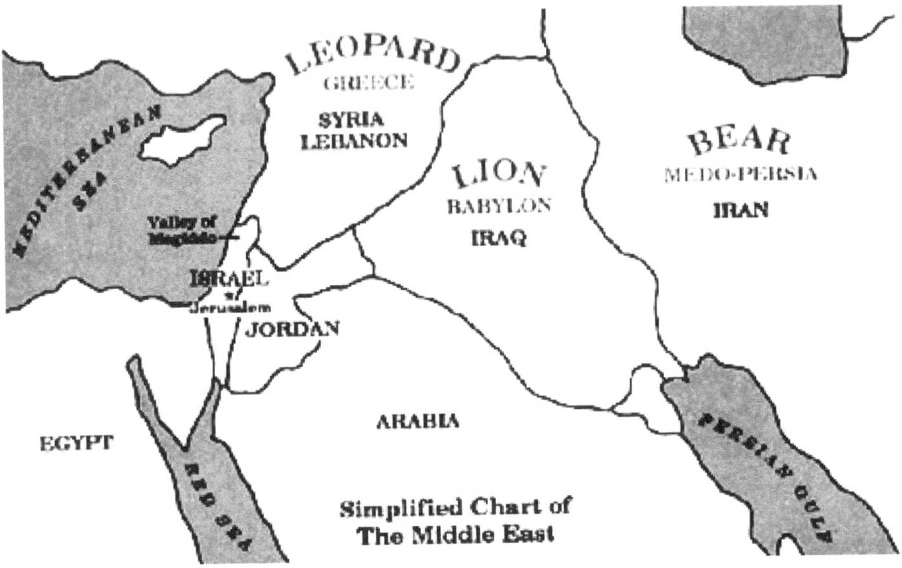

It is worth noting that there is one power that dominates this entire region. It is a power that hates the Jewish nation. A power that has tried and continues to try and destroy the Jewish nation. A people who are theologically deposed to irradicate the Jews. A theology that denies Jesus is the Son of God which is one of the signs of the Antichrist.

There is one such power that fits every aspect. It is Islam, which is not only a religion, but a way of life and a political religion. Could the Antichrist use this hatred for the Jews and the theology that drives this hatred? It seems more likely that this is out prophecy will play out.

The other details of the "Beast from the Sea" as well as his henchman the "Beast from the earth" also known as the false prophet we have dealt with in detail in chapter 3 of this book.

5. THE BEAST FROM THE ABYSS REVELATION 11:7; 17:8; 19:9

What kind of an individual will the Antichrist be?

Will he be just another human being like say Hitler who was an ordinary human being, but no doubt highly demon possessed? People who knew the inside working of the Nazi party, were aware that they were involved with the occult. Regarding Hitler himself, those close to him said that he seemed a very different person once he got to the stage and belted out his speeches. What caused ordinary German people who are like any other people, to not feel any kind of remorse when they massacred on an industrial scale the Jewish population, including little innocent children. What kind of spell was he able to cast upon the youth of the nation who followed after him as though he was some kind of Messiah?

Satan has used many such instruments in the history of mankind to further his goal. But in the last days he will empower with his authority and throne, a very wicked ruler who will terrorize and rule the nations of the earth. This evil dictator will be unlike any previous agent of Satan.

We get a glimpse of the Antichrist in chapter seven of Daniel.

DANIEL 7:24

24 *As for the ten horns, out of this kingdom ten kings will arise; and another will arise after them, and he will be different from the previous ones.......*

This "little horn" or the Antichrist will be different from the other kings. He will be a different kind of king. We get more information about this vile ruler from the book of Revelation.

In chapter nine of the book of Revelation the Apostle John saw a vision of a star that falls from heaven to earth. This fallen star has the key of the bottomless pit. The fallen star refers to a fallen angel who is in league with Satan. This fallen angel then opens up the bottomless pit which is the Abyss. Smoke comes out of this pit and out of this smoke come demons which look like locusts.

The demonic beings have king over them, the angel of the abyss.

REVELATION 9:11

11 *They have as king over them, the angel of the abyss; his name in Hebrew is Abaddon, and in the Greek, he has the name Apollyon.*

We do encounter this demoniac being in the book of Revelation.

While the evil one is frantically trying to get his final assault on the people of God accomplished through his agent the Antichrist, the living God is also at work. God sends his two witnesses to witness to the world that only the true God who is the creator of all things is to be worshipped. They have the authority to call down fire from heaven. They are given power over the sky so that they can stop the rain from falling during the days of their prophecy. They can also turn the waters into blood and strike the earth with every plague as often as they desire.

They will prophecy God's warning for a period of twelve hundred and sixty days (three and a half years). The important fact is that their ministry coincides with the same time as the rule of the Antichrist who also rules for three and a half years.

But at the end of this period, the "Beast that comes from the abyss" will kill them.

REVELATION 11:7

7 When they have finished their testimony, the beast that comes up out of the abyss will make war with them, and overcome them and kill them.

We know that the Antichrist is ruling at this time. This is the period of the great tribulation which will be for a time of three and a half years. The two witnesses sent by God will be in direct opposition and confrontation with the Antichrist. So why does the Bible tell us that the "beast from the Abyss" kills the two witnesses at the end of the three and a half years.

Are these two entities, two separate beings?

Or are they the same entities but given two different names.

The next clue we have about the beast from the Abyss is in Revelation chapter seventeen. In this chapter we have the "beast from the earth" who is renamed as the "Scarlet beast" on whom is a woman seated named "Mystery Babylon". We know that the "Scarlet beast" is the same entity as the "Beast from the Sea" as their details are similar.

1. Both beasts were dead and now are alive. *Rev 17:8*
2. The people of the earth will marvel that this beast has returned. *Rev 17:8*
3. Both beasts receive allegiance from ten kings. *Rev 17:12-13*
4. Both beasts are destroyed. *Rev 17:8*

The interesting part is that the Bible also mentions that this "Scarlet Beast" has come from the abyss. There is no doubt. The "Beast from the Abyss", the "Beast from the sea" and the "Scarlet beast" are the same person.

These are different names given to the same agent of the evil one; the Antichrist.

The Antichrist is not a normal human being. He is a fallen angel who will come from the bottomless pit which is the abyss.

THE RELIGIOUS AFFILIATION OF THE ANTICHRIST

The Bible gives us more information about this evil dictator. Can we get the religious affiliation of the power that will exert itself in the last days?

In chapter seventeen of the book of revelation we encounter this entity once again. This time the Bible calls him "The Scarlet Beast". A woman who is adorned with great wealth is seated on the scarlet beast. This woman blasphemes God and is wickedly immoral. She is the one who has persecuted and killed the people of God.

REVELATION 17:3-6

[3] *And he carried me away in the Spirit into a wilderness; and I saw a woman sitting on a scarlet beast, full of blasphemous names, having seven heads and ten horns.* [4] *The woman was clothed in purple and scarlet, and adorned with gold, precious stones, and pearls, holding in her hand a gold cup full of abominations and of the unclean things of her sexual immorality,* [5] *and on her forehead a name was written, a mystery: "BABYLON THE GREAT, THE MOTHER OF PROSTITUTES AND OF THE ABOMINATIONS OF*

THE EARTH." [6] *And I saw the woman drunk with the blood of the saints, and with the blood of the witnesses of Jesus.*

Who is this woman and how is the scarlet beast connected to this woman?

The "Scarlet beast" is the same as the "Beast from the sea" who is the Antichrist. *(Rev 17:8)*

- This beast had been defeated in the past but has now returned. *(Rev 17:8)*
- This beast has come out of the abyss. *(Rev 17:8)*
- This beast has seven heads and ten horns *(Rev 17:3)*
- It is a beast that blasphemes God. *(Rev 17:3)*
- This beast will be worshipped by those who do not know God.
- This beast will receive an allegiance from ten kings
- This beast will be destroyed

But we do get more information about this entity.

[9] *Here is the mind which has wisdom. The seven heads are seven mountains upon which the woman sits,* [10] *and they are seven kings; five have fallen, one is, the other has not yet come; and when he comes, he must remain a little while.* [11] *The beast which was, and is not, is himself also an eighth and is one of the seven, and he goes to destruction.*

[12] *The ten horns which you saw are ten kings who have not yet received a kingdom, but they receive authority as kings with the beast for one hour.*
[13] *These have one purpose, and they give their power and authority to the beast.*

The seven heads are seven mountains.

The seven mountains are seven kingdoms.

The woman sits on these seven kingdoms. Which are these seven kingdoms?

The Bible tells us that five had already fallen during the time that the apostle John was writing.

One kingdom was ruling during the time John wrote the book of Revelation.

We know that Rome was the ruling power during the time John wrote these words.

The five kingdoms that tried to destroy the people of Israel earlier, were Egypt, Assyria, Babylon, Medo-Persia and Greece. There is one common factor for these kingdoms. All of them ruled over and attempted to destroy the people of God, the nation of Israel.

But John then goes on to write that another kingdom would come after Rome. This kingdom would last for a while. This is the Ottoman Empire that controlled this area after the eastern wing of the Roman empire which was renamed as the Byzantine Empire. Though the Ottoman Empire persisted for 600 years, it succumbed to what most historians describe as a long, slow decline, despite efforts to modernize. Finally, after fighting on the side of Germany in World War I and suffering defeat, the empire was dismantled by treaty and came to an end in 1922.

The extent of this empire encompassed the entire area of all these empires except the European or the western part of the empire.

This was the seventh head.

11 The beast which was, and is not, is himself also an eighth and is one of the seven, and he goes to destruction. (Rev 17:11)

The apostle writes that there will be one last kingdom which will arise during the last days. This is the eight Kingdom. This is the kingdom of the Antichrist. The kingdom of the Antichrist will resemble the Ottoman empire in geographical extent. (The Leopard, lion and bear empire - *Revelation 13*)

This area is dominated by one power. This power is the religion of Islam which is not only a religion but also a political religion that seeks complete domination. It has a history of violent force which played a very real part in its growth.

Let's summarize the list of the kingdoms that John wrote about.

The five kingdoms that had fallen	- Egypt Assyria Babylon Medo- Persia Greece
The kingdom that existed at that time	- Rome
The kingdom that had not yet come	- Ottoman empire under Islam
The eight kingdom that would be revived	- The kingdom of the Antichrist

Are the people who follow Islam expecting someone, who fits the description of the Antichrist in the Bible as their end time Messiah. It is quite astonishing and this is something that we need to be aware about. The following information has been out in the open yet rarely discussed in the church at large. In fact, the popular view is that the Antichrist will come from Europe. However, the location of the kingdom of the Antichrist in the Bible is the Middle east, and not Europe.

Just like the study on the "End Times" is part of our endeavor to understand the future, the followers of Islam are also keenly awaiting their own Messiah called the Mahdi. It is intriguing as to how the hero of the Bible is the villain in Islam. And the villain of the Bible is the hero in Islam.

The following information is derived from Islamic sources.

There are **three Signs** for Muslims of the end of History - Each is a Man.

1. THE MAHDI – ISLAMIC MESSIAH

After reviewing the various Islamic traditions and opinions of the Muslim scholars, let's now review and walk through a list of what we have learned about the person and the mission of the Mahdi as he exists in the minds of many of the 1.8 billion Muslims worldwide.

The Mahdi is Islam's primary messiah figure. He will be a descendant of Muhammad and will bear Muhammad's name (Muhammad bin Abdullah). He will be the Caliph and Imam (vice-regent and leader) of Muslims worldwide. He will appear riding a white horse (possibly symbolic). He will have supernatural power from Allah over the wind and the rain and crops.

The Mahdi will be an unparalleled spiritual, political and military world leader who will emerge after a period of great turmoil and suffering upon the earth. He will establish justice and righteousness throughout the world and eradicate tyranny and oppression. He will possess and distribute enormous amounts of wealth and will be loved by all the people of the earth. He will lead a world revolution and establish a new world order. The Mahdi will lead military action against all those who oppose him and will invade many countries.

He will cause Islam to be the only religion practiced on the earth. He will establish the new Islamic world headquarters from Jerusalem. According to Islamic sources he will rule for seven years (possibly as much as eight or nine).

He will make a seven-year peace treaty with a Jew of priestly lineage. He will obtain some previously undiscovered biblical manuscripts with which he will use to argue with the Jews and cause some Jews to convert to Islam. He will also re-discover the Ark of the Covenant from the Sea of Galilee, which he will bring to Jerusalem.

He will conquer Israel for Islam and lead the "faithful Muslims" in a final slaughter/battle against the Jews.

2. THE ISLAMIC "JESUS"

Muslims revere Jesus (whom they call Isa) as the Masih or Messiah.

In Islamic eschatology, the Mahdi will arrive at the same time that Isa returns. He is a prophet.

Isa will descend to earth in Syria, east of Damascus, dressed in yellow robes, and will assist the Mahdi, who will rule over the world for seven years (or, in some Islamic traditions, nine or 19 years). He will come back on the wing of two angels who flew him down to meet the gathering of the army of the Mahdi.

He will pray to the Mahdi- call him "Lord."

He will make a pilgrimage to Mecca and will establish world- wide Sharia law.

He will be the greatest Muslim Evangelist.

He will reveal to the Christians that they were deceived and that he never really died for their sins.

He will shatter crosses, and abolish the tax on "non-Muslims" because there won't be any people who practice any other faith.

At the end of the Mahdi's rule, there will be a day of Judgment for the entire human race.

He will kill the "Islamic Anti-Christ."

The parallels between the biblical Antichrist and the Mahdi of Islam are chilling. Both are associated with the end times and the Judgment. Both are said to possess political, military and religious power, and head up a one-world religion. The Mahdi will force all non-Muslim people to convert to Islam. Like the Antichrist, the Mahdi will establish Jerusalem as his capital, from which he will rule the Earth.

3. THE ISLAMIC "ANTI-CHRIST"

He is called "DAJAL"- the great deceiver. He comes on a mule to earth and is blind in one eye. He is an Infidel but who also does miracles.

He claims to be Jesus- "The son of God" and will attempt to stop the Mahdi and the "true Jesus". But the "Islamic Jesus" will kill him.

Although some of the above points do not concur with the Biblical description of Jesus, some key elements regarding the persona of Jesus are included here.

WHAT CAN WE LEARN FROM THIS?

1. The Biblical Jesus is the Islamic "Anti-Christ"
2. The Biblical Anti-Christ is the Islamic "Redeemer"
3. The Biblical "False Prophet" is the Islamic Jesus.

This does fit the Biblical narrative too, but in reverse. Is this all-mere coincidence?

It is important to remember that the Muslims are sincere and most of them are like people of other religions. But we would be naïve if we do not know the reality of the reason why so many hold on to the ideology of militant Islam. Islam is not just a religion but also a political religion. There is no division between the state and religion.

WE NOW NEED TO IDENTIFY "MYSTERY BABYLON"

In the book of Revelation, we have two cities that represent two different powers.

Both cities are represented by women who are radically different.

THE TWO WOMEN OF REVELATION

1. The pure bride- New Jerusalem
2. The filthy prostitute –Mystery Babylon

THESE ARE THE TWO CITIES.

One represents a rebellious city.

The other is the "city of God"

In order to understand what this mysterious city represents; we will have to go right to the beginning of the Bible and trace its origin. We will have to go to the book of Genesis where we first encounter the city of Babylon.

Babylon was the first city that was built after the flood of Noah. This city was built by a man called Nimrod. (Genesis 10:8-12) It is widely accepted that Nimrod instigated a rebellion against God by building a city whose tower reaches to the heavens.

His name also can be translated as "to rebel".

THE TOWER OF BABEL.

The city that challenged God was the city of Babylon or Babel built on the banks of the Euphrates River. He wanted to build the tallest building in the world. Nimrod wanted to build a building that reached up- to the heavens, but had been built by human hands.

Nimrod gathered the people of the Earth to build a tower. Since he was building in Mesopotamia and no stone was available, he built it out of bricks (made out of clay). They built a stepped tower, a man-made mountain.

God dealt with this rebellion by confusing their language. People spoke in different languages and could not understand each other and sounded like they were babbling. That's where the word Babel came from. But Nimrod went beyond just trying to build a tower to challenge God. There was something more sinister going on.

According to ancient Egyptian and Babylonian traditions, Nimrod's mother was Semiramis. Sometimes Semiramis is referred to as the mother of Nimrod and sometimes as his wife, leading to the belief that Nimrod married his mother. She was the queen of Babylon and High Priestess of this Babylonian cult religion. She became known as the mother of God, the mother of Heaven and the Queen of Heaven.

Tradition suggests that Nimrod died a violent death. One tradition records that a wild animal killed him. Another tradition suggests that Shem who was the great grandson of Noah killed Nimrod as he led people into the occult and idolatry.

According to these traditions, Semiramis who rose to greatness because of her son, was presented with a difficulty when her son died. She pronounced him to be a god, so that she herself would become a goddess. She became the high priestess of the babel religion and the founder of all mystery religions as well as a goddess. Nimrod became the sun god and Semiramis become the Queen of Heaven and a moon goddess. When Nimrod died, Semiramis had to maintain her grip & power over the people in Babylon. She then gave birth to an illegitimate son named Tammuz who she claims was the reincarnation of Nimrod, and through this she was able to subdue the people of Babylon.

The symbol of this ungodly religion system that was propped up by Satan to defy God, is the sun and the half moon. Every false religion has the same starting point – Babylon.

MYSTERY BABYLON

[3]*And he carried me away in the Spirit into a wilderness; and I saw a woman sitting on a scarlet beast, full of blasphemous names, having seven heads and ten horns.* [4] *The woman was clothed in purple and scarlet, and adorned with gold, precious stones, and pearls, holding in her hand a gold cup full of abominations and of the unclean things of her sexual immorality,* [5] *and on her forehead a name was written, a mystery: "BABYLON THE GREAT, THE MOTHER OF PROSTITUTES AND OF THE ABOMINATIONS OF THE EARTH."* [6] *And I saw the woman drunk with the blood of the saints, and with the blood of the witnesses of Jesus.*

- She was seated on the scarlet beast -Revelation 17: 3
- The woman was clothed in great riches - Revelation 17:4
- She had a cup full of immorality and abominations- Revelation 17:5
- Her description - "Babylon the great, - Revelation 17:5
    - The mother of harlots
    - And of the abominations of the earth.
- She was drunk with the blood of God's people - Revelation 17:6
- The woman is the great city which rules over the kings of the earth - Revelation 17:8

The woman represents false religion that is a direct rebellion against the Creator. Men began to worship creation rather than the Creator.

The Babylon of the book of Revelation is not the same city. It represents the same spiritual climate that was present at the real city of Babylon. The Babylon of Revelation is a coastal city with ships passing by. The book of Revelation warns people to flee from Babylon as its destruction is near.

The Babylon of Revelation is the city which now rules over the kings of the earth. Babylon is a prostitute. She has sold a lie to the nations and has profited by her trade. She is drunk on the blood of the saints. It is a city of pleasure and money.

WHICH CITY COULD REPRESENT THE BABYLON OF REVELATION?

The identity of this city has been a difficult task. Suggestions regarding its identity range from Rome to Washington D.C to Mecca as well as other cities.

Some believe it is modern Germany. Germany is making an effort to become the financial capital of Europe at Frankfurt. They have built a vast new stock exchange. Outside the exchange is a huge golden calf. In the bank headquarters a massive painting around the wall is the picture of hell. Every known sin is portrayed in this painting which is full of demons gloating over their victims. There are bronze figures standing near the cash counters all totally naked in and in objectionable poses. Businesses control the nation.

IS IT ROME?

The Catholic Church with its headquarters in the Vatican, has a dark history. It has used terrible violence instigated against disciples of Jesus. It has done all these in the very name of God whom they have claimed to represent. It is a historical reality that during the dark ages, it actively sought to keep the Bible from the hands of ordinary people. Entire groups of people were massacred under the guidance of the Popes if they did not submit to the dictates of the Catholic Church. Historical data point to the number of people killed during the inquisitions from fifty to a hundred million Christians.

Rome is the first city which Peter calls Babylon. (1 Peter 5:13)

COULD BABYLON BE IN THE MIDDLE EAST?

The Middle East is responsible for the martyrdom of many Christians. The religion of Islam is responsible for the annihilation of a vast multitudes of Christians. The city of Mecca is the head- quarters of the Islamic world. There are some interesting facts about Mecca.

- Mecca means "Mother" (Babylon is called "Mother of harlots")
- Mecca is the center for radical Muslims who regularly slaughter Christian populations.
- The key figures of the Babylonian system of worship are the sun, moon and stars.
- The Islamic flag is the half crescent moon and the sun.
- The believers were beheaded for the testimony of Jesus.
  Beheading is still followed in Saudi.

We have more clues about this city in the Bible.

THE BEAST DESTROYS BABYLON -REVELATION 17:15-18

And he said to me, "The waters which you saw where the harlot sits, are peoples and multitudes and nations and tongues. And the ten horns which you saw, and the beast, these will hate the harlot and will make her desolate and naked, and will eat her flesh and will burn her up with fire.

For God has put it in their hearts to execute His purpose by having a common purpose, and by giving their kingdom to the beast, until the words of God will be fulfilled.

The woman whom you saw is the great city, which reigns over the kings of the earth."

The ten kings will give their authority to the Beast. This alliance will then attempt to make war with the Lamb of God who is Jesus. But will utterly fail against Jesus who is the King of Kings.

But before this they will destroy the city of Babylon.

She is also called the Harlot. So now we need to identify this city who the Bible calls "mystery Babylon. We get to know more about this city in chapter eighteen of Revelation.

REVELATION 18: 9-13

"And the kings of the earth, who committed acts of immorality and lived sensuously with her, will weep and lament over her when they see the smoke of her burning, 10 standing at a distance because of the fear of her torment, saying, 'Woe, woe, the great city, Babylon, the strong city! For in one hour your judgment has come.'

11 "And the merchants of the earth weep and mourn over her, because no one buys their cargoes any more— cargoes of gold and silver and precious stones and pearls and fine linen and purple and silk and scarlet, and every kind of citron wood and every article of ivory and every article made from very costly wood and bronze and iron and marble, [13] and cinnamon and spice and incense and perfume and frankincense and wine and olive oil and fine flour and wheat and cattle and sheep, and cargoes of horses and chariots and slaves and human lives.

The reasons this city called Mystery Babylon could be Mecca are quite plausible.

- John saw this city in a wilderness (Revelation 17:3)
- Saudi has used oil to control countries and the merchants of these countries have bowed down to her wish because of the supply of oil. Saudi has also pushed the Jihadist agenda with the revenue received from oil.
- The biggest shipping lane in the world is the Red Sea, and Mecca sits right on these trade routes. If Mecca is burned, the city can be easily seen from these shipping lanes.
- The commodities that are traded are in line with the products purchased by the oil rich kingdom. Human slaves are still bought and sold in this kingdom.
- The manner in which the people mourn over the destruction of this place is typically a Middle Eastern custom i.e., throwing sand over their heads in mourning. (Revelation 17:19)

THE CITY OF NEOM IN SAUDI

The kingdom of Saudi is gradually moving away from radical Islam from the last few years. The oil wealth through which the Saudi's pushed their agenda of Wahabi Islam is under threat as the world moves away from its dependance on oil.

This shift from oil has meant that Saudi Arabia needs to look ahead to a future which is weaned of its dependance to oil. The young de facto ruler Prince Salman has begun to restructure the nation. At the center of his plan to modernize the nation is a city called NEOM which is already under construction. He plans to make this the place the most advanced hi tech city in the world. The city will be built using trillions of dollars and the infrastructure planned is unlike anything that the world has seen.

But in order to make this place a reality, Prince Salman knows that the nation will have to put aside the stone age laws of the past and modernize the nation. The laws have been changed considerably in the last few years to accommodate a more liberal society.

Part of the plan is also to do away with almost 90% of the Hadiths. (*Hadiths are explanations and interpretations of Muhammad's living example.*)

This is already causing a great deal of anger in the Muslim world and it stand to reason that the Anti-Christ will target this city as it seen as a deviation from the radical bent of militant Islam.

THE DESTRUCTION OF BABYLON:

God does not destroy Babylon. But God will judge this city which is the epicenter for the Babylonian religion. The rulers who are controlled by Babylon rebel against Babylon and it is they who destroy Babylon.

The identification of the Scarlet Beast kingdom leads us to the conclusion that the leader would be a propagator of Islam. The question does arise as to why the Beast and his allies destroy this religious city.

A little bit of Islamic eschatology will help us in uncovering this fact. According to the Koran and the Hadith, the end would only come when the Islamic Messiah who is called the Mahdi would arrive to rule over the world. The Mahdi would destroy Mecca and establish his capital from Jerusalem; He will rule over the world and establish the complete domination of Islam.

Are all these facts mere coincidences or should they be taking with a pinch of salt. The reality is that in the spiritual battle between good and evil, we should be aware of these factors. The Bible has always been found reliable in every area of life especially prophecy.

CHAPTER 5

THE "ABOMINATION OF DESOLATION"

When Jesus taught the disciples about the last days prior to His return, he gave them the signs they were to watch out for. He gave them signs that he described as birth pangs. Just as birth pangs are progressive in nature, so will these signs be progressive in nature. The greatest intensity of pangs happens just before the birth of a child. In the same way, these signs will increase as the return of Jesus draws near.

SIGNS IN THE WORLD

1. Wars and kingdoms against kingdoms (Matthew 24:6-7)
2. Famines and earthquakes (Matthew 13:8)
3. Plagues (Luke 21:11)

SIGNS IN THE CHURCH

1. Deception
2. Persecution
3. A falling away and betrayal

4. False prophets will mislead many
5. The love of many will go cold due to lawlessness
6. The Gospel will be preached to the Nations

All these signs are generic in nature because one cannot measure these signs to know when the last days have arrived. However, Jesus gave one particular sign which no one can miss. He called it "the Abomination that causes desolation".

When would this incident take place?

Jesus pointed out that this incident would take place in Judea in the holy place. There is something very interesting about this prophecy. A little while earlier the disciples had been admiring the Jewish Temple and like every Jew were very proud of this magnificent building.

When Jesus warned them that the Temple would be destroyed in such a way that not a stone would remain upon each other, they were puzzled. Jesus then gave them the signs that they should watch out for so that they would know when this destruction would take place. Jesus also warned the nation that Jerusalem would be surrounded by armies that would desolate the land. He told them that Jerusalem would be surrounded and razed to the ground along with the temple.

Jesus warned that that the Jewish people would go into exile into all the nations. Then he said something astonishing. He prophesied that Jerusalem would be under control of Gentile powers until the time of the Gentiles was fulfilled.

The city of Jerusalem was completely destroyed by the Romans in 70 A.D. A million Jews were killed and an equal number were sold as exiled into other nations as slaves. From that day when the Temple was torn down there is no ritual sacrifice being offered by the Jews. Although many of them have returned to Israel and even have control over Jerusalem, they still do not have a temple. The "time of the gentiles" is over and the "times of the end" has begun.

LUKE 21:24

...... for there will be great distress upon the land and wrath to this people; and they will fall by the edge of the sword, and will be led captive into all the nations; and Jerusalem will be trampled underfoot by the Gentiles until the times of the Gentiles are fulfilled.

In this prophecy of Jesus, we also get to understand that although the people of Israel would be exiled and dispersed from the land, they would also be revived and return to their land. Another clue we have is that is that the final sign about the return of Jesus, given by Jesus is the "abomination of desolation". Where would this sign occur? Jesus told us it would happen in Judea. The end time focus will once again be the nation of Israel.

MATTHEW 24:15-22

15"Therefore when you see the ABOMINATION OF DESOLATION which was spoken of through Daniel the prophet, standing in the holy placelet the reader understand— 16 then those who are in Judea must flee to the mountains. 17 Whoever is on the housetop must not go down to get things out of his house. 18 And whoever is in the field must not turn back to get his cloak. 19 But woe to those women who are pregnant, and to those who are nursing babies in those days! 20 Moreover, pray thatwhen you flee, it will not be in the winter, or on a Sabbath. 21 For then there will be a great tribulation, such as has not occurred since the beginning of the world until now, nor ever will again. 22 And if those days had not been cut short, no life would have been saved; but for the sake of the elect those days will be cut short.

Let us try and grasp what Jesus has prophesied.

1. This is a confirmation of the prophet Daniel's prophecy in Daniel chapter twelve.
2. This abomination will be connected to Judea and the holy place.
3. The tribulation will be so severe that once the people see this abomination, they are warned to run away as soon as possible.

4. This tribulation will be so severe that such trouble has never occurred since the beginning of the world until then, nor would ever happen again.
5. God will intervene and cut short this time otherwise none of the elect will survive.

DANIEL'S PROPHECY ABOUT THE END TIMES

The prophet Daniel wrote a lot about the end of days. Daniel was exiled to Babylon as a teenager in 606 B.C. With unshakable faith in the God of his forefathers and an undivided heart to serve his God, Daniel was raised to prominence in the courts of the king of Babylon. The kingdom of Babylon survived for until 538 B.C. This kingdom was then defeated by the Medo- Persian empire.

Daniel continued to thrive under king Darius and then under king Cyrus who were Medo- Persian kings. In the third year of the reign of king Cyrus, Daniel receives a message through a vision that greatly disturbs him. He goes on a fast to seek the lord. On the twenty first day of his fast an angelic being visits Daniel and tells him that the message is with regards to the future of the people of Israel in the last days.

DANIEL 10:14

Now I have come to explain to you what will happen to your people in the latter days, because the vision pertains to the days still future."

The vision is then explained in Daniel chapter 12.

DANIEL 12:1-3

Now at that time Michael, the great prince who stands guard over the sons of your people, will arise. And there will be a time of distress such as never occurred since there was a nation until that time; and at that time your people, everyone who is found written in the book, will be rescued. 2

And many of those who sleep in the dust of the ground will awake, these to everlasting life, but the others to disgrace and everlasting contempt. [3] *And those who have insight will shine like the glow of the expanse of heaven, and those who lead the many to righteousness, like the stars forever and ever.*

Daniel writes that the nation would go through such a time of distress that has never occurred nor would ever occur again. When would this happen? This would happen immediately prior to the resurrection of the dead. We know from the New Testament that this resurrection happens at the return of Jesus. This is also the time when the book will be opened which has the record of every human being. The rewards and judgement will be in accordance to the way each individual lives their life.

The Lord has given the nation of Israel, a sign that they would warn them that the great tribulation was at the door. He called this incident "the abomination of desolation". But what exactly is this sign. Does the Bible have record of a similar event that has happened in the history of the nation?

THE GREEK EMPIRE AND THE UNGODLY KING

After the death of Alexander, the kingdom wrangled and fought for about 20 years and then it was divided into four kingdoms.

The four generals were:

Cassander - ruled over Greece and its region.

Lysimachus - ruled over Asia Minor.

Seleucus - ruled over Syria and Israel's land.

Ptolemy - ruled over Egypt.

Two of these kingdoms were short lived and the two that remained were ruled by Seleucus Nicator, and Ptolemy. They are referred to as King of the North (Seleucus) and King of the South (Ptolemy).

ANTIOCHUS EPIPHANES

The arose a king from the Seleucid empire who was not only extremely cruel but in every way an enemy of the people of God. This king was Antiochus Epiphanes also called the "mad king". The world has never seen a viler person than Antiochus Epiphanes. A full description of this person is written in great detail in the Bible:

Daniel 11:21 *"He will be succeeded by a contemptible person who has not been given the honor of royalty. He will invade the kingdom when its people feel secure,*

This contemptible ruler will be successful in war; will be shrewd, and cunning.

Daniel 11:28 *The king of the North will return to his own country with great wealth, but his heart will be set against the holy covenant. He will take action against it and then return to his own country.*

Antiochus returns to Syria with riches that he had gained in his exploits, but he hated the Jews and his heart was set upon doing all the damage possible to Jerusalem. He hated the word of God and tried to destroy its manuscripts and adherents.

THE ABOMINATION THAT CAUSES DESOLATION

Daniel 11:31 *"His armed forces will rise up to desecrate the temple fortress and will abolish the daily sacrifice. Then they will set up the abomination that causes desolation.*

Antiochus came against the Jewish high priest Onias after arriving in Jerusalem with a big army. He took the city by force, plundered the city and killed a multitude of Jews. He compelled the high priest to flee to Egypt and set up another high priest.

He desecrated the Temple and put a stop to the sacrifices that were being offered at the Temple. The daily sacrifices were stopped for a period of three and a half years. He sacrificed swine's flesh upon the altar and was opposed by the Jews for this act. He robbed the Temple of the gold that was kept at the Temple. He does worse than anyone before him when he sets up an idol of his god Jupiter Olympus in the Temple and sacrifices swine on God's altar.

He compelled the Jews to stop following the Law of God and forbade the circumcision of the Jewish children. Anyone who opposed him was brutally killed. Any Jew who supported him was rewarded and there were some who turned over to his side so that they could receive favors from him.

Not only did he stop the Jews from worshipping their God, but Antiochus also built temples in honor of his gods whom he forced the Jews to worship. Many succumbed to his persecution, but others stood to oppose him.

He destroyed the books of the Law wherever he could find them. It is important to note that by this time, the entire Old Testament had already been translated into Greek and was called the "Septuagint".

Daniel 11:36 *The king will do as he pleases. He will exalt and magnify himself above every god and will say unheard-of things against the God of gods. He will be successful until the time of wrath is completed, for what has been determined must take place.*

Antiochus exalted himself, and magnified himself above every god and uttered incredible blasphemies against the Eternal God of Heaven. Why would God allow this arrogant, blasphemer, homosexual, pedophiliac villain to continue on such a killing spree?

The Lord judged this king who died in very strange circumstances. God brought this impious wretch to a dreadful end. He was stricken with a disease unlike any mortal man ever received. The disease caused a foul odor to emanate from his body so that no man wanted to be near him. He could not stand the foul odor himself.

Worms were coming from his body. His flesh was dropping off. He was in agony with pain in his bowels. He begged God like a pauper for mercy. This vile man promised to be a Jew and amend his way if God would withdraw his hand from him, but the just judgment of God never let him off the hook.

THE SHADOW OF THE ANTICHRIST

Antiochus is a shadow of the Antichrist. In the way that Antiochus troubled the nation of Israel, so will the Antichrist trouble the people of God in the last days. The epicenter of his wrath will be the nation of Israel, but his evil designs will also extend to the people of God all over the earth. The similarities between Antiochus Epiphanes and the Antichrist are startling.

The coming "Man of Sin" is the very manifestation of Satan in human form. He will receive a kingdom and authority from Satan. His goal will be to usurp the worship that is due to God alone, and cause all men in every nation to bow down to himself. He will use every aspect of economic sanctions, terror and the use of deception to make mankind bow to his will.

THE SIMILARITIES BETWEEN ANTIOCHUS AND THE ANTICHRIST DANIEL 8:23-26

Verse	Scripture	Fulfillment
8:23	In the latter time of their kingdom:	The prophecy in this passage reads equally true of both Antiochus and Antichrist. This is an example of a prophetic passage that has both a *near* and *far* fulfillment.
8:23	Having fierce features	Antiochus Epiphan es was known for his cruel brutality. This will also be true of the coming Antichrist.
8:23	Who understands sinister schemes... through his cunning	Antiochus was known for his flattery and smooth tongue. The coming Antichrist will also use deceit to get his way.

8:24	His power shall be mighty, but not by his own power	Antiochus Epiphanes was empowered by Satan and allowed by God. The same will be true of the coming Antichrist.
8:24	He shall destroy the mighty, and also the holy people	Antiochus Epiphanes not only destroyed his enemies, but also harshly persecuted the people of God. The coming Antichrist will also destroy and persecute.
8:25	He shall cause deceit to prosper	Both the rule of Antiochus Epiphanes in the past and of the Antichrist in the future are marked by deceit. *The coming of the lawless one is according to the working of Satan, with all power, signs, and lying wonders, and with all unrighteous deception among those who perish, because they did not receive the love of the truth, that they might be saved (2 Thessalonians 2:9-10)*
8:25	He shall exalt himself in his heart	The coins of Antiochus Epiphanes were inscribed with this title: THEOS EPIPHANIES meaning, "God manifest." The coming Antichrist will also exalt himself: *So that he sits as God in the temple of God, showing himself that he is God (2 Thess 2:4).*

8:25	He shall even rise against the prince of princes	Though Antiochus Epiphanes hated the people of God and fought against them, it was because he really hated God. The same will be true of the coming Antichrist, who will hate the Jews as well as those who follow Jesus, because he hates God.
8:25	Broken without human means	History tells us that Antiochus Epiphanes died of disease, not by the hand of man. In a similar way no *man* will defeat the coming Antichrist, but the hand of Jesus will strike him down (Revelation 19:20).

THE SHADOWS OF THE "ABOMINATION OF DESOLATION"

1. Antiochus Epiphanes — 2nd Century B.C
2. The Romans under Titus — 70 A.D
3. The Antichrist — Unknown future

The first time the Jewish Temple was desecrated and the abomination happened during the reign of Antiochus Epiphanes. He brought forth great evil upon the Jewish people. He was the shadow and type of the evil dictator who will persecute the people of God in the end times. His persecution was very localized mainly surrounding Jerusalem.

The second time the Jewish Temple was desecrated was when the Romans under the general Titus surrounded Jerusalem in 70 A.D. The Romans destroyed Jerusalem and the Temple completely. Over a million Jews were killed and a very large number were sold as slaves. Jesus had wept over the city and prophesied that it would be brought down.

And Jesus said to them, "Do you not see all these things? Assuredly, I say to you, not one stone shall be left here upon another, that shall not be thrown down." Matthew 23:37-24:2

In 135 A.D, the Roman Emperor Hadrian had another 500,000 Jews massacred during another Jewish revolt. Emperor Hadrian believed the source of Jewish rebellion was their faith, so he executed Jewish scholars, prohibited the Torah and the Hebrew calendar, and burned the sacred scroll on the Temple Mount.

In an attempt to completely erase Jewish history from the land, Emperor Hadrian renamed the province of Judea "Syria Palestina."

Jews were banned from entering Jerusalem on pain of death. The second time of the abomination that caused the desolation of Jerusalem was far reaching, and its effect on the Jewish people went far beyond Jerusalem, as they were exiled and scattered among the nations.

Both these occasions are but shadows of the final desolation that will take place under the Antichrist. He will severely persecute the Jewish nation after declaring himself as God. He will rule from Jerusalem while he seats himself at the very place where the Temple was situated.

The evil arm of the Antichrist will go far beyond the boundaries of Israel and reach to the entire world. His target will be the people of God who are both the people of Israel, as well as the followers of Jesus. Since he receives authority and a throne from Satan himself, he will also do the bidding of his master.

REVELATION 12:17

17 So the dragon was enraged with the woman, and went off to make war with the rest of her children, who keep the commandments of God and hold to the testimony of Jesus.

CHAPTER 6

IDENTIFYING THE "ABOMINATION THAT CAUSES DESOLATION"

THE JEWISH TEMPLE

The Temple Mount is by far one of the most holy sites in the entire world. It is revered and honoured by the Jews, Christians, and Muslims. It is here that God tested Abraham to offer his own son Isaac as a sacrifice. That is why this place is holy to the Jews. Solomon built the first Temple as per the plans laid out by his father David in this very location.

This Temple was destroyed by the Babylonians in 586 B.C. The Jewish people were then exiled in Babylon.The initial returnees from Babylonian to Jerusalem, led by one Sheshbazzar, began to reconstruct the temple but were forced to abandon the project. A second group of returnees, under the direction of the appointed provincial governor, Zerubbabel, completed and dedicated it. According to the book of Ezra, construction of the second Temple was called for by the Persian king Cyrus, and began sometime between 538 and 536 B.C.

This second temple stood (though robbed and desecrated several times) for about 570 years. Herod the great began a vast renovation and expansion of the temple in 20 BC which continued for 46 years. The renovation was large enough and significant enough that the result is referred to as

"Herod's Temple", though it was still the "second temple", not a third one. It was finally destroyed and burned by the Romans in 70 A.D.

Today millions of Jewish people come to the western wall of the Temple Mount to pray.

To the Christians, the Temple Mount is sacred because it is the place Jesus was dedicated to the Lord; it is where He taught; and where He overturned the money tables. He even prophesied against the Temple. It is also where many of the apostles taught about Jesus in the book of Acts.

Finally, to the Muslims, the Temple Mount is considered the third most holy site in Islam. In Muslim tradition it is believed that Muhammad ascended to Allah from the Temple Mount. The Dome of the Rock is a Muslim shrine that marks the location from which Muhammad ascended. Also, the famous Al-Aqsa Mosque sits at the southern end of the Mount.

This small but very sacred site has been passed from hand-to-hand over the past 3,000 years. The ancient Israelites controlled it, as have the Persians, Greeks, Romans, Arabs, Crusaders, Turks, British, Jordanians, and now the modern Israelis.

So, if the modern Israelis control East Jerusalem, how do the Jordanian's have control of the Temple Mount? In 1967 during the Six-Day War the Jordanians, who had control of the West Bank and East Jerusalem, attacked Israel with the help of Syria and Egypt. The Israelis pushed the Jordanians out of the West Bank and as a result took East Jerusalem and the Temple Mount.

After the dust settled from the Six-Day War, Israeli Prime Minister Levi Eshkol returned the authority of the Temple Mount to the Islamic Waqf. The Waqf are the Islamic guardians of Muslim holy sites; they watch over them and make sure they are being managed properly. Levi Eshkol returned the Temple Mount to the Islamic Waqf as a gesture of peace to the Arab world.

THE SIGNIFICANCE OF THE TEMPLE MOUNT IN THE GREAT TRIBULATION

2 THESSALONIANS 2:1-4

Now we ask you, brothers and sisters, regarding the coming of our Lord Jesus
Christ and our gathering together to Him, 2 that you not be quickly shaken
from your composure or be disturbed either by a spirit, or a message, or a
letter as if from us, to the effect that the day of the Lord has come. 3 No one
is to deceive you in any way! For it will not come unless the apostasy comes
first, and the man of lawlessness is revealed, the son of destruction, 4 who
opposes and exalts himself above every so-called god or object of worship, so
that he takes his seat in the temple of God, displaying himself as being God.

The Bible reveals that this Temple Mount will be the epicenter of geopolitics in the last days. The focus will shift to Israel and then Jerusalem and then to the Temple Mount. This will take place when the Antichrist whom the apostle Paul names as "the man of lawlessness", exalts himself as God and demands worship of all the nations of the earth. This evil dictator rules from the Temple Mount. This is what the Bible calls "the abomination that causes desolation"

We now know what the abomination means. But what is the "desolation"?

Jesus spoke about a desolation that would take place of Jerusalem when the nation of Israel failed to recognize the Messiah. Their leaders condemned him to death on a cross. The nation paid a very heavy price for this rejection. The Romans under general Titus destroyed both the Temple and the city of Jerusalem. The Jews witnessed a desolation of their city and nation for almost two thousand years.

The Jews have recovered and are back in the land of their forefathers. Just as prophesied, God has brought them back to their land. The dried bones in the valley have now become a great army. The cities of Israel have revived and the nation has become a shining example to the world that it is possible to thrive in spite of tremendous obstacles. It has been no less than a miracle that Israel is considered a rich country with the eighth most powerful army in the world, although it has no natural resources like oil and gas that empowers their very rich neighbors.

But there is major trouble ahead for this nation. Jesus confirmed the prophecy of Daniel regarding the "great tribulation" that would take place in Israel just prior to the end of the age. How severe would this tribulation be? Let us see what Daniel prophesied first and then what Jesus confirmed.

DANIEL 12:1-2

"Now at that time Michael, the great prince who stands guard over the sons of your people, will arise. And there will be a time of distress such as never occurred since there was a nation until that time; and at that time your people, everyone who is found written in the book, will be rescued. 2
And many of those who sleep in the dust of the ground will awake, these to everlasting life, but the others to disgrace and everlasting contempt.

DANIEL 12:9-11

9 *And he said, "Go your way, Daniel, for these words will be kept secret and*
sealed up until the end time. 10 *Many will be purged, cleansed, and refined,*
but the wicked will act wickedly; and none of the wicked will understand,
but those who have insight will understand. 11 *And from the time that the*
regular sacrifice is abolished and the abomination of desolation is set up,
there will be 1,290 days.

Jesus our Lord and Saviour also gave this warning to the Jewish nation. We understand from the scriptures that although Jesus specifically warned that Jerusalem and the nation of Israel would be the epicenter of the great tribulation, the Antichrist would target all the people of God everywhere on the earth.

MATTHEW 24:15-21

15 "Therefore when you see the ABOMINATION OF DESOLATION which was spoken of through Daniel the prophet, standing in the holy place—let the reader understand— 16 then those who are in Judea must flee to the mountains. 17 Whoever is on the housetop must not go down to get things out of his house. 18 And whoever is in the field must not turn back to get his cloak. 19 But woe to those women who are pregnant, and to those who are nursing babies in those days! 20 Moreover, pray that when you flee, it will not be in the winter, or on a Sabbath. 21 For then there will be a great tribulation, such as has not occurred since the beginning of the world until now, nor ever will again.

Jesus confirmed what the prophet Daniel prophesied about the great trouble that will come upon the nation of Israel. Jesus said that such great trouble was never experienced in the past nor will any such trouble happen after that. This is a very strong statement. Many nations have faced much horror in the history of their people. History has recorded many incidents of such profound acts of barbarism and devastation. Yet Jesus warned that this time of trouble that would come upon the people of Israel in the last days would be worse than anything that has ever been dealt with any nation. This is a chilling prophecy.

The "Abomination of Desolation" would be the sign that the time of the great tribulation had begun. What other information does the Bible give us with regards to this incident?

In the book of Revelation chapter thirteen, we are introduced to the evil incarnation of Satan himself. He is named "the beast from the Sea". He is Satan's anointed henchman who will receive his throne and authority to rule on behalf of the evil one. This man of lawlessness will receive assistance by another henchman of Satan who the Bible calls "the Beast from the earth". Another name given to this satanic individual is "the false prophet"

The false prophet will be empowered to do signs and wonders. He will deceive the nations of the earth through these spectacular acts so much so that he is even able to call down fire from heaven. He will demand that the people of the earth bow down and worship the Antichrist. To ensure this worship, he will install an image of the Antichrist and demand that everyone on the earth bow down to this image. If anyone does not bow down and worship this image he will be executed.

Where will this image of the Antichrist be installed? This image will be installed in the holy place. When the Bible talks about this holy place it is with regards to the most holy place which was in the Jewish Temple. Since the Jewish temple was on the Temple Mount, it stands to reason that the Abomination that causes desolation would also take place on this very site.

REVELATION 13:1-17

[11] Then I saw another beast coming up out of the earth; and he had two
horns like a lamb, and he spoke as a dragon. [12] He exercises all the authority
of the first beast in his presence. And he makes the earth and those who live
on it worship the first beast, whose fatal wound was healed. [13] He performs
great signs, so that he even makes fire come down out of the sky to the earth
in the presence of people. [14] And he deceives those who live on the earth
because of the signs which it was given him to perform in the presence of
the beast, telling those who live on the earth to make an image to the beast
who had the wound of the sword and has come to life. [15] And it was given to
him to give breath to the image of the beast, so that the image of the beast
would even speak and cause all who do not worship the image of the beast
to be killed. [16] And he causes all, the small and the great, the rich and the
poor, and the free and the slaves, to be given a mark on their right hands
or on their foreheads, [17] and he decrees that no one will be able to buy or to
sell, except the one who has the mark, either the name of the beast or the
number of his name.

CHAPTER 7

HOW LONG WILL THE GREAT TRIBULATION LAST

This topic has been discussed and debated endlessly in the church. Scholars are divided on this very important topic. There are mainly two points of view.

One group believes that the book of Revelation is largely a symbolic book and the literature in it seeks to bring about the truth that good will ultimately triumph over evil. It is therefore assumed that there is no time frame of the cosmic battle.

The other group believes that although the book of Daniel as well as the book of Revelation do have symbolic material, they are prophetic in nature with actual characters and real events that have taken place through history but the climax is yet to come. The climax will be the great tribulation and the return of Jesus the Messiah in order to restore the earth to the righteous rule of God.

Among the second group however there is an ongoing debate about the length of the tribulation period. The most popular view is that this period will last for a total of seven years. The seven-year period is extracted from a prophecy of Daniel.

DANIEL 9:24-27

*24 "Seventy weeks have been decreed for your people and your holy city, to
finish the wrongdoing, to make an end of sin, to make atonement for guilt,
to bring in everlasting righteousness, to seal up vision and prophecy, and to
anoint the Most Holy Place. 25 So you are to know and understand that from
the issuing of a decree to restore and rebuild Jerusalem, until Messiah the
Prince, there will be seven weeks and sixty-two weeks; it will be built again,
with streets and moat, even in times of distress. 26 Then after the sixty-
two weeks, the Messiah will be cut off and have nothing, and the people of
the prince who is to come will destroy the city and the sanctuary. And its
end will come with a flood; even to the end there will be war; desolations
are determined. 27 And he will confirm a covenant with the many for one
week, but in the middle of the week he will put a stop to sacrifice and grain
offering; and on the wing of abominations will come the one who makes
desolate, until a complete destruction, one that is decreed, gushes forth on
the one who makes desolate."*

A PERIOD OF "SEVENTY TIMES SEVEN"

Daniel the prophet receives this word while he was in Babylon. The Israelites had messed up their relationship with God for hundreds of years. The lord had sent many prophets who admonished them and gave them warning after warning to repent. But the Israelites continued in their rebellion. Finally, God took them to task as he had repeatedly warned them and sent them into exile. The southern kingdom of Judea was defeated by Babylon. The Jewish Temple was destroyed and the people went into captivity in Babylon.

Daniel knew that the captivity would last for a period of seventy years as the prophet Jeremiah had written. When the seventy years were nearly done, Daniel began to seek the Lord. The Lord then revealed this message of "seventy weeks" to the prophet.

God had ordained a period of seventy weeks or a period of 490 years to give the people of Israel another chance. But this time they would not only be restored into their land but also get back their Temple. This time they would get an opportunity to meet with their Messiah.

It was a time frame that God would give the Jewish people to repent, receive their Messiah and take their place as the favored people among the nations of the Earth. At stake was also the city of Jerusalem. The Messiah would come at a specific time in history and would accomplish these things for his people.

DANIEL 9:24

"Seventy weeks have been decreed for your people and your holy city,

- to finish the transgression,
- to make an end of sin,
- to make atonement for iniquity,
- to bring in everlasting righteousness,
- to seal up vision and prophecy and
- to anoint the most holy place.

DANIEL 9:25

So you are to know and discern that from the issuing of a decree to restore and rebuild Jerusalem until Messiah the Prince there will be seven weeks and sixty-two weeks;

it will be built again, with plaza and moat, even in times of distress.

In the passage, God told Daniel (through His angel)

That He was giving the Jews one last chance to repent of their sins,

To reconcile with God,

To prepare for their coming Messiah.

The "weeks" were not ordinary days at all, but sevens of years. Every day of these 70 weeks represented a prophetic year and we can prove it through historical events.

The 490 years would be broken into three parts.

7 weeks or 49 years

62 weeks or 434 years

1 week or 7 years

From the issuing of the decree, to the coming of the Messiah there would be a period of "Seven weeks" and "Sixty-two weeks".

The Angel explained to Daniel that the city and its streets would be rebuilt, but in difficult times. The Jews would know the starting date from the decree that would announce the rebuilding of the city. If we scroll back through history, we find that there were four decrees that were announced by the Medo- Persian kings with relation to Jerusalem.

When would the date of the 490 years begin?

INITIATOR	PASSAGE	DATE	PARTICULARS OF THE DECREE
Cyrus	**Ezra 1:1-4**	**539 B.C.**	Allowed the Jews to return home and rebuild their Temple. The work ceased because of false allegations (Ezra 4:6-13)
Darius	**Ezra 6:8-12**	**520 B.C.**	Allowed the Jews to complete the rebuilding of the Temple.
Artaxerxes	**Ezra 7:11-26**	**457 B.C.**	Gave authority to Ezra to lead the nation in the Laws of God.
Artaxerxes	**Nehemiah 1**	**445 B.C.**	Gave permission to Nehemiah to rebuild the walls of Jerusalem.

Ezra was given this mandate in the 7th year of Artaxerxes.

Allowing for his ascension year, this Persian king began his reign in 464 B.C.

This places the king's decree to Ezra around 457 B.C.

(464 B.C minus 7 years = 457 B.C.)

We find Ezra also alludes to possibly been given permission in his prayer not only to rebuild the Temple but also to build the walls of Judah and Jerusalem.

EZRA 9:9

"For we are slaves; yet in our bondage our God has not forsaken us, but has extended loving kindness to us in the sight of the kings of Persia, to give us reviving to raise up the house of Our God, restore its ruins and to give us a wall in Judah and Jerusalem."

WHEN WAS THE MESSIAH REVEALED TO THE JEWS?

God was giving not only the time frame, but also what the Messiah would do for His people. If we follow the timeline, we come to the year 27 A.D. The very year John the Baptist began preaching in the wilderness. The very year John baptized Jesus and declared that Jesus was "the lamb that takes away the sins of the world"

DANIEL 9:25

So you are to know and discern that from the issuing of a decree to restore and rebuild Jerusalem until Messiah the Prince there will be seven weeks and sixty-two weeks;

LET'S DO SOME MATH

7 x 7 = 49 years

62 x 7 = 434 years

The total would be 483 years

The calculation should be **457 – 483 – 1 = 27 A.D.**

Remember not to count year zero going from B.C. to A.D. because this will produce a one-year error. These 483 years gives us the time frame from the issuing of the decree to rebuild Jerusalem, till the Messiah is presented to the people of Israel. This is the exact date when John the Baptist began his public ministry. Jesus had begun His public ministry at the age of 30.

HISTORICAL EVIDENCE.

Using the historical evidence of the starting date of 457 B.C. for the decree to rebuild Jerusalem and the fifteenth year of the reign of Tiberius Caesar, (Luke 3:1) while allowing for the one year of joint rule with Augustus, gives us the identical date of 27 A.D. verifying it is correct.

THE LAST WEEK

There remains however another period of "one week" or a period of seven years.

What would happen in these last seven years?

Here is where it gets interesting.

A very popular opinion is that the last seven years are in the future. Accordingly, the last seven years are called the tribulation period. Israel will make a covenant with the "Anti-Christ" for a period of seven years. The "Anti-Christ" will allow the Jewish Temple to be built on the holy site. Sacrifices and offering would resume just like they were offered during the time of the first two Temples. In the middle of the seven years, the Anti-Christ will break his covenant with the people of Israel, and after declaring himself as God would persecute them. The period of the great persecution will last for the remaining three and a half years.

THE DIFFICULTY WITH THIS VIEW

There is a difficulty with this position. The problem is that we have to assume that the seventy-week period is broken up. We do not have the mandate from the scriptures to take this liberty.

Let us take a couple of examples. When the Israelites were told that they would be in the wilderness for forty years, it was exactly forty years at a stretch. Similarly, when the Israelites were sent into captivity for seventy years into Babylon, it was in accordance with the warning given to Judah by the prophet Jeremiah. In the same way when the Lord gave Israel a period of "seventy weeks" it is to be taken in continuity.

WILL THE THIRD TEMPLE BE BUILT?

Could a third Temple be built in Jerusalem in the last days? For this to take place, it would take an extraordinary change in the hearts of around 2 billion Muslims to allow the place where the Al- Aqsa Mosque is located, to be substituted by a Jewish temple.

Could the Abraham accords that are initiated to bring peace between the nation of Israel and the Arab neighbors lead to such a situation. It seems very improbable at the moment, but geo-political compulsions may make room for such a possibility. The Jews however, could choose an alternate location and construct their Temple.

Daniel the prophet did warn that the tribulation will begin when the sacrifices are stopped and the "Abomination that causes desolation" will take place. In order for the sacrifices to be stopped it is necessary for the third Temple to be built so that the sacrifices can begin in the first place.

Some Bible teachers believe that the Antichrist will be able to bring about a settlement and allow for the building of the third Jewish temple on the temple mount itself. There are clear indications that the Anti-Christ will declare himself as God and demand worship from all mankind. Jerusalem will be the epicenter during the rule of the Anti-Christ.

WHAT WE KNOW ABOUT THE LENGTH OF THE GREAT TRIBULATION

The Bible uses a number of terms to describe the time frame of the great tribulation. Let us list each reference we have, for this difficult time that the people of God will be subjected to.

1. A time, times and a half time -Daniel 7: 25
2. A time, times and a half time -Daniel 12:7
3. A time, times and a half time -Revelation 12:14
4. One thousand two hundred- and sixty-days -Revelation 11:3
5. One thousand two hundred- and sixty-days -Revelation 12:6
6. Forty-two months -Revelation 13:5

Each of these references in the scriptures are in context of the great tribulation that will come upon the people of God. Each reference is the same time frame – three and a half years. In each reference, the Antichrist under the authority of Satan will inflict a time of severe testing upon the people of God with the nation of Israel as the focus.

CHAPTER 8

THE MARK OF THE BEAST AND 666

IDENTIFYING THE BEAST AND HIS NUMBER -666

The question regarding the meaning of the number 666 or the "number of the Beast" has both fascinated as well as terrified Christians through the centuries.

This number has been attributed to many individuals. Some believe it refers to the Roman Emperor Nero who severely persecuted the Christians in the early church. Some say it points to the head of the Roman Catholic Church who is the Pope. There is a recorded history of how the Roman Catholic Church has persecuted Christians who refused to submit to the authority of the Pope.

Some say it is Hitler while others say Obama and the list goes on.

THE ORIGIN OF THE NUMBER 666

In order to get a better understanding of the number 666, it is advisable to find out from the past if there is a reference to this number. Since this number is in connection with the act of worship, it is a good starting point.

Only the living God is worthy of worship. He has created the heavens and the earth along with all life, and His power upholds all things. God has also created the Angelic beings.

One among them rebelled against God. The Bible gives him many names. He is Satan.

The Bible also calls him "The Deceiver", The Serpent", The Dragon" etc. He became filled with pride because of the beauty that God had created him with. He desires to be worshipped in the way God is worshipped. From the very beginning he has tried to deceive mankind and sought worship. He has succeeded in blinding the eyes of most of mankind in this regard.

From the very beginning, Satan has used deception as his favorite tool to lure man. He started this deception in the garden of Eden. Once he gained dominion after getting Adam and Eve to sin against God, he has continued throughout human history. He was able to get mankind to shift their focus of worship from the creator to the creation.

The advent of nature worship began right after flood of Noah. When men began to increase after the flood, they found a leader in a man called Nimrod. The meaning of the word Nimrod means "One who rebels. He began building cities and the first city he named "Babylon". The meaning of this word means "To confuse or to mix". It was the mixing of the truth with a lie. This was also the first city that was built after the flood during the time of Noah.

It culminated with the building of the Tower of Babel. The tower was in the form of an ancient building structure called Ziggurats. The top of these towers was the place where the worship of the starry hosts took place.

It was the starting point of all false religion. This was the worship of created beings and created objects rather than the worship of the Creator. This is where the worship of the sun the moon and the stars began. Any kind of worship that is not presented to the true God, is worship of Satan.

Every false religion has its root and source from Babylon. The religious system of Babylon comprised of not one but many gods and goddesses. In the astrological religion of Babylon, every god had his sacred number or numbers which were often used in place of the god's name. These numbers indicated the god's place and power among the astrological gods...

Because the Babylonians saw their gods as being predominantly evil, they feared that one of them may strike them down sometime. This is why they made these amulets with a 6 * 6 matrix with the numbers 1 through 36 on them, which are called numeric matrixes magic squares today.

NUMBER OF THE BEAST AMULET.

The design of the amulets was to protect them from a god striking them down using his magic power so the amulets had to be as powerful as possible. In order to increase its power, they arranged these numbers in such a way that the sum of any given row, column or diagonal was 111, and therefore the sum of all six rows or all six columns was 666.

6	32	3	34	35	1
7	11	27	28	8	30
19	14	16	15	23	24
18	20	22	21	17	13
25	29	10	9	26	12
36	5	33	4	2	31

THE BABYLONIAN RELIGIOUS SYSTEM

In this system of worship, they had 36 supreme gods, which included the sun god, which they believed to be the father of all the other gods and so was supreme over all.The Babylonians believed that numbers had power over their gods they worshiped so they assigned numbers to their gods so that they could have power over them.

They did this by counting their gods and assigning a consecutive number to each of the 36 lesser supreme gods, and then added up these numbers (from 1 to 36) and assigned the sum to the sun god. The sun god was assigned number 1 as it was the father of all gods and thus was also the male deity. The moon god was assigned number 2 and of course was the female deity. The gods numbered from 3 through 36 were considered the children of the sun and the moon god.

THE "MARK" ON THE HAND OR FOREHEAD

How is the mark of the beast placed on someone's right hand or forehead? (Revelation 13:16)

Is the mark some kind of chip that is inserted in the body? This technology exists, and there is increasing acceptance that this kind of technology will help monitor all human activity. While this has advantages in health issues and regulation of finances, this will also lead to an end to human freedom to quite an extent. Since economic activities will be subjective to whether an individual takes the mark of the beast or not, it is very plausible that the Antichrist will use this technology to force people to worship him. But should we look at this technology as the "mark of the beast" or is there something deeper at play?

WE HAVE AN EXAMPLE WHEN GOD COMMANDED ISRAEL TO OBEY HIM

When God brought the Israelites out of Egypt, He gave them the Law through Moses. Regarding his commands to the nation of Israel regarding his Word, God said: "Bind them as a reminder on your hand, and they should be like a headband on your forehead." (Deuteronomy 11:18)

This meant that the Israelites were not to literally mark their hands and foreheads, but that God's words would guide all their actions and thoughts.

Likewise, rather than being something literal such as a 666 tattoo, the mark of the beast symbolically identifies those who let the political and religious system of the Antichrist rule their lives. Those with the mark of the beast place themselves in opposition to God.

REVELATION14:9-12

*9Then another angel, a third one, followed them, saying with a loud voice,
"If anyone worships the beast and his image, and receives a mark on his
forehead or on his hand, 10 he also will drink of the wine of the wrath of
God, which is mixed in full strength in the cup of His anger; and he will be
tormented with fire and brimstone in the presence of the holy angels and in
the presence of the Lamb. 11 And the smoke of their torment ascends forever
and ever; they have no rest day and night, those who worship the beast
and his image, and whoever receives the mark of his name." 12 Here is the
perseverance of the saints who keep the commandments of God andtheir
faith in Jesus*

CHAPTER 9

WHERE WILL THE CHURCH BE DURING THE GREAT TRIBULATION

The very thought of the great tribulation sends visions of horror among Christians who understand the ramifications of that dark hour. The Church is not new to persecution. From its very inception it has experienced great persecution. Starting from the very beginning the Church had to swim against the flow. It is tough trying to be the light in a world, that that is very comfortable in the dark.

THE HISTORY OF PERSECUTION OF THE CHURCH

If they hate Me, they will hate you too.... These words of Jesus have proved true over the entire age of the church. Whether overtly with violence, or with attempts to silence the Church through laws that prohibit the words of the Bible being spoken in public, the opposition to Christ continues.

The first opposition to the church came from the Jews who did not accept Jesus as the Messiah. Since the first Christians were largely Jewish converts, the opposition came from the Jewish leadership who saw this as a challenge to their faith.

the prospect of being left behind in a world that has such an apocalyptic future.

BIBLICAL BASIS OFFERED FOR THIS POSITION AND THE QUESTIONS THAT ARISE

It is important to note that all Biblical doctrine must be taken in its right context. The entire council of scripture is needed before we come to any meaningful conclusion on any subject, especially in important matters like the return of our Lord Jesus Christ.

Let us take each point one at a time.

1. There are scriptures that say Jesus is coming 'quickly' so therefore it is inferred that every generation be ready since his return is about to happen.

   The word quickly is used very often. It is quick, but not in human terms. it has already been 2000 years since Jesus spoke these words. While two thousand years is a long time for us, it is not very long for God who is not constrained by time.

   A day for the Lord can be thousand years and a thousand years can be a day.

2. Jesus spoke about His return with the phrase "like a thief in the night. It is said that "The day of Christ" is the day that Jesus takes His church to be with Him, also popularly called the "rapture". It is proposed that Jesus comes just before the great tribulation to take the Church to heaven. This will be a secret event and the people of the earth will be unaware of the return of Jesus.

   "The day of the Lord" which is a day when Jesus returns to judge the earth. This will be a public display of the power and the glory of God. It is assumed that these are two different events with a gap of either seven years or three and a half years.

   In reality the Bible does not distinguish between this day. For example, the two harvests that are symbolic of the righteous being gathered to Christ and the judgement of the wicked by Christ in the book of Revelation are simultaneous events. (Revelation 14:14-20)

3. Inference from the expectation of the early church - 'This generation shall not pass away' until all these things are fulfilled. So, since it is taught that early church expected this so it is inferred that Jesus can come at any time.

   Did the early church expect him any moment?

   - Jesus said take the gospel to the ends of the earth. How could they expect him any moment?
   - Jesus predicted that Peter would be crucified in his old age. He would be carried where he did not want to go- crucified
   - John was told he would die an old man.
   - They hoped that he would come back soon but they were not expecting Him to arrive soon.

4. Absence of the word 'church' from Rev chapter 4 to 16 through the time of the great tribulation. It is assumed that since the word church is missing, the church will not be there.

   The bible regularly uses the word "Saints, Elect" for the Church. So, the argument is not valid.

   There are 6 epistles that use the word elect but not Church. (2 Tim, Titus, 1 Peter, 2 Peter, 2 John, Jude 1 epistles). Jude uses saints but not church.

   It is reasonable to ask as to why would Jesus give us so much information of the great tribulation, if we won't be around? It does not add up.

5. The tribulation is God's wrath: we are not children of wrath.

   Since we are God's children we cannot go through wrath.

[9] *For God has not destined us for wrath, but for obtaining salvation through our Lord Jesus Christ,* [10] *who died for us, so that whether we are awake or asleep, we will live together with Him.* (1 Thessalonians 5:9)

But the bible also mentions that at the moment, his wrath is being poured out on the world.

The book of Revelation also points out that some Christians will have been put to death.

What does the Bible reveal to us regarding the wrath of God. The Bible communicates that the "Day of the lord" is also the "wrath of God". Let us read a few passages in the Bible that clarifies this issue.

ZEPHANIAH 1:18

Neither their silver nor their gold will be able to save them on the day of the LORD's wrath."
In the fire of his jealousy the whole earth will be consumed,
for he will make a sudden end of all who live on the earth.

ISAIAH 2:17-19

The arrogance of man will be brought low and human pride humbled; the LORD alone will be exalted in that day, and the idols will totally disappear.
People will flee to caves in the rocks and to holes in the ground from the fearful presence of the LORD and the splendor of his majesty,when he rises to shake the earth.

REVELATION 6:16-17

[16] *They called to the mountains and the rocks, "Fall on us and hide usfrom the face of him who sits on the throne and from the wrath of the Lamb!* [17] *For the great day of their wrath has come, and who can withstand it?"*

6. The Church is the bride of Christ. God will never allow the bride of Christ to go through the tribulation.

   The argument is very weak. The Church which is the bride of Christ existed from the very first generation of Christians. We know from history that the early church was persecuted. Through out the last two thousand years, a very large number of disciples have been killed for their faith. In many regions of the earth, persecution is a daily occurrence in the lives of many believers. The bride of Christ of Jesus Christ has endured through many tribulations.

   What then can we learn from the above discussion? This point of view does not bear scrutiny. We must be aware that,there is not a single direct verse that says "God's people will not go through tribulation". These views are taken from texts that seem to imply or infer from certain scriptures.

THE SECOND VIEW – THE CHURCH WILL BE ON EARTH DURING THE TRIBULATION

The basic teaching of this view is that Jesus comes after the great Tribulation. There is no secret rapture at the beginning of the tribulation. This a significantly different world view that brings into focus two sides – preparing to escape the Tribulation or preparing to endure.

Let us have a look through the vantage points that propel this perspective.

1. The pre- tribulation rapture is not found in the Bible. One can infer it from types and shadows and use this method to infer certain positions. For example – Noah did not suffer because of the flood as he was in the Ark, and God did not send the flood until he and his family were in the safety of the ark. A lot of these metaphors are used to justify this position. But the reality is that there is not a single verse in the Bible that declares directly that the church will not be on earth during the Tribulation.

There are however some scriptures that directly point out to the rapture taking place after the tribulation. In Matthew 24, Jesus said that the return of Jesus and the gathering together of the saints will be after the tribulation.

2. IT IS NOT FOUND IN CHURCH HISTORY

The first time we hear about the teaching that the church would escape the great tribulation was in the 19th Century. We have the details of how this teaching began. This teaching was largely condemned by the leaders of that time. But some latched onto it. Nelson Darby (Brethren) and Dr. C.L. Scolfield were very influential figures in modern theology. The Scolfield study Bible was one of the most popular Bible especially for the footnotes provided on every topic. This Bible was the most popular until quite recently.

The "Left Behind" series became popular literature among Christians and this teaching spread like wild fire. The picture of people disappearing while their clothes get left behind is enough to make people anxious.

However, we do not have any such teaching before 1830 A.D. This is a relatively new teaching which does not do well under scrutiny.All throughout church history, people anticipated that Jesus would gather the church on the same day that He comes to judge the earth. There is an obvious danger that this teaching may prepare the people of God to wait for an escape, rather than be prepared for endurance. This may set people up for confusion, delusion and offense.

3. THIS TEACHING IS MOSTLY TAUGHT IN THE WEST

The West has had a remarkably free society, with the freedom to practice and propagate any religion. This freedom is under tremendous threat recently. Yet for the most part, everyone is still allowed to decide the faith of their own choice. Outside the West, many Christians routinely face persecution and the ability to choose your faith is always under intense scrutiny. In places like China, parts of Africa and the Middle East, Christians regularly lose their lives for their faith. Even in secular countries like India and other south east Asian countries, the pressure to conform to traditional religions is growing.

In this context, the West which does not face the kind of persecution like the other nations is very comfortable with the idea that the Church will escape the great tribulation. The West has been largely shielded from any tribulation and therefore finds fertile ground for this teaching.

In other countries of the world, where persecution is a part of life, this teaching finds some ground mainly because it is taught in the West. Much of the Church today is already living in tribulation. It is not the great tribulation yet- that will come later. The people living outside the West like the Middle East, parts of Africa and Asia are not preparing for the great escape. They are already experiencing persecution at many levels.

4. JESUS NEVER TAUGHT THE DISCIPLES TO ESCAPE BUT ENDURE.

When Jesus spoke to His disciples, he warned them that they would have much to endure. Even from the beginning, He alerted them about what would happen as they followed Him. They would be persecuted and even have to testify before kings and governors. Jesus promised them that they would not be without help as he would continue to strengthen them. Then he encouraged them to endure and thus receive the reward of their salvation.

That has been the pattern of Christian history. The Church of Jesus Christ has always been at odds with the world. The world in turn hates true Christianity as it hates Jesus. The world hates Jesus as it is under the dominion of Satan. This confrontation between the kingdom of light and the kingdom of darkness will continue until the end of this age.

LUKE 21:12-18

12 "But before all these things, they will lay their hands on you and persecute
you, turning you over to the synagogues and prisons, bringing you before
kings and governors on account of My name. 13 It will lead to an opportunity
for your testimony. 14 So make up your minds not to prepare beforehand to
defend yourselves; 15 for I will provide you eloquence and wisdom which
none of your adversaries will be able to oppose or refute. 16 But you will be
betrayed even by parents, brothers and sisters, other relatives, and friends,
and they will put some of you to death, 17 and you will be hated by all people
because of My name. 18 And yet not a hair of your head will perish. 19 By
your endurance you will gain your lives.

THE COMING OF JESUS WILL DO TWO THINGS:

1. The Righteous will be delivered.
2. The wicked will be punished.

THE WRATH OF GOD VERSES THE WRATH OF SATAN

IMPORTANT CHARACTERISTICS OF THE WRATH OF SATAN

The tribulation is the Devil's persecution against the righteous. The Antichrist is given authority and a throne from Satan himself. The worship of the antichrist will be in essence, the worship of Satan. Satan will empower his agents the Antichrist and the false prophet, to deceive the nations of the earth. The entire earth will fall in line with the dictates of the Antichrist.

Satan has always attempted to get mankind to join in his rebellion against God. When anyone resisted his attempts, his strategy has been to employ persecution against the people of God. Not only does he have a very well-established kingdom of darkness on the earth, but he also has access to heaven, where he accuses the people of God before the throne of God. The Bible reveals that in the last days, there will be a war in heaven between the angels of God led by Michael the archangel and Satan and his fallen angels. Satan will be defeated and expelled from heaven. This will greatly enrage him and he will descend with the goal of destroying the people of God. This is what will spark the great tribulation.

REVELATION 12:12

Therefore rejoice, you heavens and you who dwell in them!
But woe to the earth and the sea, because the devil has gone down to you!
He is filled with fury, because he knows that his time is short."

REVELATION 13:5-10

5 *The beast was given a mouth to utter proud words and blasphemies and to exercise its authority for forty-two months.* 6 *It opened its mouth to*

blaspheme God, and to slander his name and his dwelling place and those who live in heaven. [7] It was given power to wage war against God's holy people and to conquer them. And it was given authority over every tribe, people, language and nation. [8] All inhabitants of the earth will worship the beast—all whose names have not been written in the Lamb's book of life, the Lamb who was slain from the creation of the world.
[9] Whoever has ears, let them hear.
[10] "If anyone is to go into captivity, into captivity they will go.
If anyone is to be killed with the sword, with the sword they will be killed."
This calls for patient endurance and faithfulness on the part of God's people.

IMPORTANT CHARACTERISTICS OF THE WRATH OF GOD:

The wrath of God is against the wicked. When the patience of God finally runs out against rebellious mankind, it will lead to judgement. Just as it happened in the days of Noah, so it will take place at the return of Jesus. It will be the day of reckoning when mankind has to face his creator.

OBADIAH 1: 15

"The day of the LORD is near for all nations.
As you have done, it will be done to you;
your deeds will return upon your own head.

ZEPHANIAH 1:14-15

The great day of the LORD is near; near and coming quickly.
The cry on the day of the LORD is bitter;
the Mighty Warrior shouts his battle cry.
[15] That day will be a day of wrath—
a day of distress and anguish, a day of trouble and ruin,
a day of darkness and gloom, a day of clouds and blackness—

The Lord alone will be exalted on that day.

ISAIAH 2:10-12

Go into the rocks, hide in the ground from the fearful presence of the LORD
and the splendour of his majesty!
11 *The eyes of the arrogant will be humbled and human pride brought low;*
the LORD alone will be exalted in that day.
12 *The LORD Almighty has a day in store for all the proud and lofty,*
for all that is exalted (and they will be humbled),

GOD'S WRATH ENDS SATAN'S WRATH

Six thousand years of human history has made one thing very clear. Mankind is lost without God. Not the gods who are made in the imagination of sinful man, but the true and living God. People who say that they can't believe in God because of the cruelty that they see in the world, miss out a very important point. The cruelty and the mess in the world are not because God is not in control, but because God will not take away the freedom of choice given to mankind. History has shown that man has very rarely chosen good. The rebellious streak and the desire to dominate everyone else no matter what the cost, has only brought about pain and suffering in a world that has gone downhill morally.

Evil men, spurred on by evil instincts have dominated for most of human history. Like in the garden of Eden, Satan has lured men to do his bidding while promising external power but internal carnage. The target of the evil one has always been those who follow God, and resist him. Throughout history, the people of God have been persecuted by the axis of evil men, goaded on by the serpent himself. The culmination of all things evil will be the time of the great tribulation.

But God has promised that there will be day of reckoning for all of His creation. The "day of the Lord" is the day when God says enough is enough. The true ruler of the realm of mankind will descend with power and glory. God will take charge over His creation completely. Jesus is the king of kings and the Lord of lords. Every knee will bow and every tongue will confess that Christ is Lord. It will be payback time for those who hate good and love evil.

2 THESSALONIANS 1:6-10

*For after all it is only just for God to repay with affliction those who afflict
you, 7 and to give reliefto you who are afflictedand to us as well when the
Lord Jesus will be revealed from heaven withHis mighty angels in flaming
fire, 8 dealing out retribution to those who do not know God and to those
who do not obey the gospel of our Lord Jesus.*

*9 These will pay the penalty of eternal destruction, away from the presence of
the Lord and from the glory of His power, 10 when He comes to be glorified in
His saints on that day, and to be marveled at among all who have believed—
for our testimony to you was believed.*

CHAPTER 10

THE DESTRUCTION OF THE ANTICHRIST

A question that perplexes many people is" why do bad things happen to good people"?

Another equally puzzling question is "why does God allow evil people to rule"?

Let us ponder on the second question. One of the beautiful gifts that God has given to the angels and even to all mankind, is freedom. Freedom to choose right or wrong, good and evil. For love to truly be expressed, freedom is very crucial. Without freedom of choice, love would be impossible.

God is love according to the Bible. Therefore,God has given freedom to the angels and to all human beings. Freedom to love Him or hate Him. Freedom to believe Him or disbelieve Him. Freedom to accept Him or reject Him. Freedom to accept His rule or reject His rule.

Some of the angels chose otherwise. The Bible gives us glimpses of what happened when one of the chief angels chose to rebel against God. He was created with great beauty and held a place of honor among the angels. But pride got the better of him and he became corrupt. His chief goal was to take the place of God. He hasn't stopped trying. The bible gives him many names such as the Serpent, the Dragon, the Deceiver, the Adversary, and the accuser of the brethren.

When God created mankind, He gave Adam and Eve a beautiful world, and everything was very good. But along with dominion over the earth, God also gave Him freedom of choice. The freedom to choose whether Adam would accept God's plan for his life or choose to go his own way. The tree of the knowledge of good and evil was in essence a chance to choose. Who would decide what is good and evil. Would it be God or man.?

This is where Satan found his opportunity. If he could convince man to reject God, he would fall into the trap laid out by Satan. He could then have man on his side and in rebellion against God. The fatal choice by Adam to go his own way trapped all the descendants of Adam and Eve in a spiral downward. Mankind lost their dominion by joining hands with the enemy of God. They did not get freedom but bondage to the evil dictator Satan.

Every evil dictator is but a shadow of the real power behind them. Human history has revealed that mankind has a great attraction towards evil. The desire for power is a trait that is common to every race among men. This desire for power and control has brought about much misery and pain for as long as we have recorded human history. The freedom that God has given mankind is often misused and it is a reflection of the choice made by Adam and Eve in the garden of Eden. Man is still trying to play God, and the consequences have been disastrous.

We have progressed much in technology and innovation to make the lives of most people much easier than the previous generations. But the important matters of a weary soul have been neglected badly. In the desire to move ahead of others, children are taught to compete and win. The external matters of money, power and fame are highlighted as achievements. But the internal matters of the soul, along with peace of mind and moral character are not given any real consideration. The result is the proliferation of people visiting psychiatrists rather than Jesus "the good shepherd" who alone can restore the soul.

THE BATTLE FOR THE SOUL

The cosmic battle has been playing out in the realm of mankind. The enemy of the souls of men, has been relentless in his pursuit of convincing mankind to join in his rebellion against God. Being the very fountain of evil, the serpent also called the dragon does not play by the books. He doesn't care about fair play or right and wrong. He hates mankind almost as much as God loves man. Having taken control of the dominion given to man, he uses every evil trick in the book to destroy those who will not join in his rebellion. He raises up puppet rulers who do his bidding and the effect is much pain and suffering.

In the genealogy of Cain and Seth who are the sons of Adam and Eve, the Bible gives us a summary of the two paths that mankind would eventually take. The path of the righteous and the unrighteous. The genealogy of Cain is recorded until Lamech. The genealogy of Seth is recorded until Noah. Both genealogies are laid out until the great flood that took place when Noah built the ark in obedience to the command of God. It is fascinating to observe how the descendants of Cain are evil while the descendants of Seth are God fearing. When the judgement sent by God resulted in the flood, only the godly survived. This is a snapshot of how eventually the history of the good and evil will conclude.

The ungodly Cain had already revealed his character when he killed his brother who had brought an offering that pleased God. Using wicked cunning, he had lured his brother to a place where he killed him. That would be the pattern of how we see mankind has come thus far. The ungodly hate the righteous and will continue to persecute those who follow God.

Although at times it seems unfair that the godly suffer at the hands of the ungodly, the Bible assures us that what happens on earth is not the end. Everyone will have to stand before the throne of God at judgement and God who is righteous and just has the final say. The reason that God seems to delay His judgement on the earth, is due to His patience with mankind. Sometimes however God's judgement is very visible and this is how it will be at the time of the Antichrist.

THE ARMIES OF THE EARTH GATHER TO CONFRONT JESUS

The Antichrist will be given a kingdom and a throne by Satan himself in the last days before the return of Jesus. He will have almost complete power over the nations of the earth and will certainly have control over the financial systems of the earth. He will declare himself as God and demand worship from everyone on the earth. The Antichrist will be allowed a period of three and a half years to rule. The Bible records that the Antichrist will wage war against the people of God and will be allowed to overcome them. The only opposition he will encounter is the two witnesses mentioned in the book of Revelation chapter eleven.

The Antichrist's henchman who is the false prophet will do great signs and wonders by which he will deceive the world. However,they will not be able to stop the two witnesses who will be anointed by the Lord to be witnesses to a world that is under the deceptive spell of the evil one.When the three and a half years are completed, the Antichrist will kill the two witnesses.

A very strange incident will take place just prior to the return of Jesus. The Antichrist will rally the armies of the nations for a great battle. This is no ordinary battle. This battle will be to confront Jesus whose return is imminent. This is a most foolish idea. To imagine that man actually has power to confront the Creator in a physical combat is nothing more than lunacy. But such is the deception that the Devil has been able to achieve towards rebellious mankind, that it is astonishing. The armies are gathered together for the battle that will take place in the north of Israel. This is the battle of Armageddon.In Psalms chapter two, this confrontation is laid out in detail. It is a panoramic view of the armies of the kings of the earth gathered together to fight against the true king of all the earth.

PSALM 2:1-6

Why are the nations restless
And the peoples plotting in vain?
2 *The kings of the earth take their stand*
And the rulers conspire together

Against the LORD and against His anointed, saying,
[3] *"Let's tear their shackles apart*
And throw their ropes away from us!"
[4] *He who sits in the heavens laughs,*
The Lord scoffs at them.
[5] *Then He will speak to them in His anger*
And terrify them in His fury, saying,
[6] *"But as for Me, I have installed My King*
Upon Zion, My holy mountain."

THE ANTICHRIST AND HIS ARMIES DESTROYED

Needless to say, it doesn't end well for the armies of the earth who have joined hands with the Antichrist. Jesus who is the "King of kings" and the "Lord of lords" will return in power and majesty. The lamb of God is also the lion of Judah. The Saviour of the earth is also the judge.

The Antichrist and the false prophet will then be thrown into the lake of fire.

Let us see where the Bible records these incidents which will soon take place.

DANIEL 7:11

[11] *Then I kept looking because of the sound of the boastful words which the horn was speaking; I kept looking until the beast was killed, and its body was destroyed and given to the burning fire.*

2 THESSALONIANS 2:8

[8] *Then that lawless one will be revealed, whom the Lord will eliminate with the breath of His mouth and bring to an end by the appearance of His coming;*

REVELATION 19:19-20

19 *And I saw the beast and the kings of the earth and their armies, assembled to make war against Him who sat on the horse, and against His army.*

20 *And the beast was seized, and with him the false prophet who performed the signs in his presence, by which he deceived those who had received the mark of the beast and those who worshiped his image; these two were thrown alive into the lake of fire, which burns with brimstone.*

THE TRAGEDY OF THE LOST

The Bible warns us about the final destination of the wicked. The first ones who are thrown into the lake of fire are the Antichrist and the false prophet. Satan who is the main antagonist in the Biblical narrative will then be locked up in the abyss for a thousand years.

During this period of a thousand years mankind will finally experience what it means to be governed by a truly righteous ruler. Jesus our Messiah will rule along with his people for a thousand years which is called the "Millennium rule of Christ".

After the thousand years is over, Satan will be released and cast into the lake of fire to join the Antichrist and the false prophet. What happens next should be of concern to every human being.

JUDGMENT AT THE THRONE OF GOD

11 *Then I saw a great white throne and Him who sat upon it, from whose*
presence earth and heaven fled, and no place was found for them. 12 *And*
I saw the dead, the great and the small, standing before the throne, and
books were opened; and another book was opened, which is the book of life;
and the dead were judged from the things which were written in thebooks,
according to their deeds. 13 *And the sea gave up the dead who were in it,*
and Death and Hades gave up the dead who were in them; and they were
judged, each one of them according to their deeds. 14 *Then Death and Hades*
were thrown into the lake of fire. This is the second death, the lake of fire.

[15] *And if anyone's name was not found written in the book of life, he was thrown into the lake of fire.*

Hell was never made for mankind. This place of weeping and gnashing of teeth was made for the Devil and his angels. God who is just, has given man every chance to choose good over evil. When men reject the grace of God and His overtly open display of his love at the cross,no one can blame God. Moreover, when people choose the kingdom of darkness over the kingdom of light, then wherever the king lives so will the people of his kingdom.

A frightening prospect for those whose names is not in the book of life.......

CHAPTER 11

THE RETURN OF THE KING

The return of Jesus will be dramatic. Jesus said it would be so spectacular that the entire world would witness his return. He will appear in great glory and splendor. Jesus gave us the signs that will precede his return. There will be signs in the sky.

MATTHEW 24:29-30

But immediately after the tribulation of those days THE SUN WILL BE DARKENED, AND THE MOON WILL NOT GIVE ITS LIGHT, AND THE STARS WILL FALL from the sky, and the powers of the heavens will be shaken. [30] And then the sign of the Son of Man will appear in the sky, and then all the tribes of the earth will mourn, and they will see the SON OF MAN COMING ON THE CLOUDS OF THE SKY with power and great glory.

BEING CAUGHT UP WITH CHRIST – THE "RAPTURE"

What a glorious union it will be when the Church will join with Christ the Saviour. Christ will ultimately return bodily, visibly, and gloriously to reign and rule with His resurrected and transformed saints forever and ever. The Church will be caught up to be with Him forever.

MATTHEW 24:31

31 And He will send forth His angels with A GREAT TRUMPET BLAST, and
THEY WILL GATHER TOGETHER His elect from the four winds, from
one end of the sky to the other.

THE JUDGEMENT OF THE UNGODLY

The Bible declares that God has a day allotted when he would judge the people of the earth. The day of the lord will be a day of terror to the enemies of the Lord. The pride of man will be humbled and the Lord will be exalted on that day. When Jesus returns, the high and mighty men of the earth will hide in fear. The Lord who has been patient with man will reveal his wrath against an evil generation.

REVELATION 6:12-17

12 And I looked when He broke the sixth seal, and there was a great
earthquake; and the sun became as black as sackcloth made of hair, and the
whole moon became like blood; 13 and the stars of the sky fell to the earth, as
a fig tree drops its unripe figs when shaken by a great wind. 14 The sky was
split apart like a scroll when it is rolled up, and every mountain and island
was removed from its place. 15 Then the kings of the earth and the eminent
people, and the commanders and the wealthy and the strong, and every
slave and free person hid themselves in the caves and among the rocks of the
mountains; 16 and they said to the mountains and the rocks, "Fall on us and
hide us from thesight of Him who sits on the throne, and from the wrath of
the Lamb; 17 for the great day of Their wrath has come, and who is able to
stand?"

THE KINGDOMS OF THE EARTH WILL BECOME THE KINGDOM OF OUR GOD

For over thousand years Christians have prayed; Thy kingdom come, thy will be done on earth, as it is in heaven. God has given glimpses of

His kingdom when that happens. Broken lives are restored, the sick are healed, and the kingdom of darkness recedes.

When God began His creation work, He first made the earth and all the stars and planets. Then God made Adam's body out of the earth. Later He breathed life breath into man, and Adam became a living soul. Adam was made of two parts: the temporary body made of the earth, and the eternal soul made from the breath of God. The temporary is seen, the eternal is unseen. Everything that God made for man was very good.

When Adam ate of the tree of the knowledge of good and evil, in essence he rebelled against God and messed things up for all his descendants. God had warned Adam that this would set the downward spiral of creation, made for man. The relation with God would be the first casualty and that is what death truly is. Mankind would slowly lose their relationship with God and that would produce spiritual death. The next casualty was that death was introduced for all living creation, and that is the death of the human body. Because the earth along with the animals and plants were under the dominion of man, everything came under the curse. From then on, the earth began to produce thorn and thistles where earlier it was all good.

In the restoration of the earth, we will see this in reverse.

The Lord began the restoration process at the cross. The "Son of God" became the "Son of Man" and lived among us. He revealed the true nature of our God and fully expressed the love that He has for all of Mankind. He paid the price for our rebellion which began at the garden of Eden. Man, now can receive the gift of salvation accomplished for us by Jesus at the cross.

Jesus' death on the cross, first brought back our spiritual resurrection. The Bible calls it being "born again". When Jesus returns, we will receive a resurrected body. It will be very different from the body we now have which is susceptible to disease and physical death. Then the earth will be restored as it was when God placed man in the garden of Eden.

The prophet Isaiah gives us a glimpse about that span of a thousand years which is popularly called the "Millennium period". This is the period after the tribulation and before the great White Throne judgment of the wicked. During the millennium, Jesus will reign as king over Israel and all the nations of the world.

ISAIAH 2:1-4

The word which Isaiah the son of Amoz saw concerning Judah and Jerusalem.

2 Now it will come about that in the last days,
the mountain of the house of the LORD
Will be established as the chief of the mountains,
and will be raised above the hills;
And all the nations will stream to it.[3]
And many peoples will come and say,
"Come, let's go up to the mountain of the LORD,
to the house of the God of Jacob;
so that He may teach us about His ways,
and that we may walk in His paths."
For the law will go out from Zion
and the word of the LORD from Jerusalem.

THE PROMISES OF GOD TO HUMANITY WILL BE FULFILLED

Those are the covenants God made with Israel that are to be fulfilled in Jesus' 1,000-year reign, but the Bible lists other promises that will be fulfilled, too.

1. For the first time in human history there will be peace on the earth. Mankind will finally have a perfect and just ruler. No longer will nations go to war against each other. Jerusalem will be the centre of all nations.

ISAIAH 2:4

4 And He will judge between the nations,
and will mediate for many peoples;
And they will beat their swords into ploughshares,
and their spears into pruning knives.

Nation will not lift up a sword against nation,
and never again will they learn war.

2. God promised Jesus He will make His enemies a footstool, and that Jesus' followers will worship Him freely.

PSALM 110 :1-3

The LORD says to my Lord:
"Sit at My right hand until I make Your enemies a footstool for Your feet."
[2] *The LORD will stretch out Your strong scepter from Zion, saying,*
"Rule in the midst of Your enemies."
[3] *Your people will volunteer freely on the day of Your power;*

3. God promised creation that the curse would be lifted.

ROMANS 8:18-23

[18] *For I consider that the sufferings of this present time are not worthy to*
be compared with the glory that is to be revealed to us. [19] *For the eagerly*
awaiting creation waits for the revealing of the sons and daughters of God.
[20] *For the creation was subjected to futility, not willingly, but because of*
Him who subjected it, in hope [21] *that the creation itself also will be set free*
from its slavery to corruption into the freedom of the glory of the children
of God. [22] *For we know that the whole creation groans and suffers the pains*
of childbirth together until now. [23] *And not only that, but also, we ourselves,*
having the first fruits of the Spirit, even we ourselves groan within ourselves,
waiting eagerly for our adoption as sons and daughters, the redemption of
our body.

4. Even animals and the earth would be restored to peace and prosperity.

ISAIAH 11:6-9

And the wolf will dwell with the lamb,
And the leopard will lie down with the young goat,
And the calf and the young lion and the fattened steer will be together;
And a little boy will lead them.
[7] *Also the cow and the bear will graze, their young will lie down together,*

And the lion will eat straw like the ox.
8 *The nursing child will play by the hole of the cobra,*
And the weaned child will put his hand on the viper's den.
9 *They will not hurt or destroy in all My holy mountain,*
For the earth will be full of the knowledge of the LORD
AS the waters cover the sea.

CHAPTER 12

PREPARING FOR THE RETURN OF THE KING

We are not given any specific dates given to us for the return of Jesus. But Jesus does give us a sign to look out for. Once we see this sign, we can know that it is the last generation. Which sign did Jesus give us as a reference? The reference was the "abomination of the desolation" and the great tribulation. This is the last generation that will live before the return of Jesus.

Jesus gave us an example from nature. He used the fig tree to illustrate this point. When the branches of the fig tree become tender and sprout its leaves, we can know that summer season is near. So also, we can know that the return of Jesus is imminent. In fact, Jesus pointed out that we should recognize that Jesus is right at the door. Then Jesus reveals his authority on the matter. Heaven and earth will pass away, but His words will not pass away.

MATTHEW 24:32-33

32 *"Now learn the parable from the fig tree: as soon as its branch has become*
tender and sprouts its leaves, you know that summer is near; 33 *so you too,*
when you see all these things,recognize that He is near, right at thedoor. 34
Truly I say to you, this generation will not pass away until all these things take place.

Can one know the day or the hour that Jesus will return? Jesus made it very clear. Not even the angels of heaven know when He will return. And then He says something that surprises a lot of people. Jesus says that He Himself does not know the date except the Father. Many people question this fact and then use it to challenge the divinity of Jesus.

To answer this question, we have to understand the Bible narrative. The Bible is not a mere collection of facts and proof texts. The Bible has a plot. The Bible has a story line. It is a love story. It is the story of a Father who loves His Son Jesus and seeks a bride for Him. Not in an earthly way, but in a divine way.

The Jewish marriage customs in Biblical times give us an insight that marriage was to be a reflection of the relationship between Jesus and his people. Those customs shed light on what Jesus has done for us, what He is doing for us and what He will do for us in the future.

1. The Father would choose a bride for His son. (John 17:6)
2. The bridegroom paid a large bride price (Ephesians 1:7)
3. There would be a marriage covenant (1 Corinthians 11:25)
4. The bridegroom goes to prepare a place for his bride. (John 14:2-3)

   In the Jewish custom, the bridegroom did not get to decide when he could come and receive his bride for the wedding. Only the father had the authority to do so.

5. The bridegroom comes to receive his bride once the father gives his approval.

Jesus is now preparing a place for us in heaven at His Father's house. He is also providing for our needs while we are still here on earth. He has also sent us the Holy Spirit to be our teacher and helper so that we can be ready for His return. The Holy Spirit is the seal of His promise and covenant with us.

THE SOCIAL AND SPIRITUAL CLIMATE JUST PRIOR TO THE RETURN OF JESUS.

While we cannot know the exact time; we can know the season of the Lord's return. What are the clues given to us regarding the social and spiritual climate just prior to the return of Jesus. Jesus gives us the example of two men in the Bible; Noah and Lot.

LUKE 17:26-30

26 And just as it happened in the days of Noah, so will it also be in the
days of the Son of Man: 27 people were eating, they were drinking, they were
marrying, and they were being given in marriage, until the day that Noah
entered the ark, and the flood came and destroyed them all. 28 It was the
same as happened in the days of Lot: they were eating, they were drinking,
they were buying, they were selling, they were planting, and they were
building; 29 but on the day that Lot left Sodom, it rained fire andbrimstone
from heaven and destroyed them all. 30 It will be just the same on the day
that the Son of Man is revealed.

In the case of both Noah and Lot, one thing was common. Most people were just not aware, or did not believe that judgement was just around the corner. They went about their daily activities oblivious to the fact that they did not have very long to live. But the spiritual climate was a complete mess. In the case of Noah's time, mankind had become very wicked. The Bible tells us that every thought and intention of man was continually wicked. Things had become so bad that even God was sorry that He had created man.

We also get a glimpse of the unseen world. The Bible tells us in the book of Genesis chapter six that the fallen angels, had begun to take human women as their wives. The result was a breed of hybrid descendants. These were the giants that we read about in the Bible. The demi gods which are found in many cultures all over the world, have their origins in this period of human history. The fallen angels had infiltrated and tried to destroy and pollute the seed of men. The result was that wickedness spread like a plague on the whole earth.

In the case of Lot, the highlight of the wickedness of men was illustrated in Sodom and Gomorrah. The spotlight was on homosexuality. It was evident that Sodom and Gomorrah were overly sexualized and in strange ways, so that the men of the cities moved around preying on other men.

We do not have to look too hard to see that our society at large is getting increasingly wicked. Everything good is despised and evil is upheld. Homosexuality and every kind of unnatural sex is not only promoted but there is pressure being exerted in multiple ways to conform to this agenda. In the age where every kind of sexual fantasies are made accessible even among little children, there is no doubt that we live in very precarious times.

JESUS HAS CAUTIONED THE CHURCH TO BE ALERT

Since we do not know the day in which our Lord will return, Jesus encouraged the church to be alert. We are to be ready as well for we do not really know the day the Master will return.

What does the Lord expect of His Church even as His return is near?

1. THE FAITHFUL AND THE UNFAITHFUL SERVANT

The Lord has offered us salvation as a gift although it cost Him dearly at the cross. Now we are coworkers in the house of the Lord. The Lord gives His people different kinds of gifts and talents so that each one can contribute in the growth of the kingdom. But the Lord does expect faithfulness, especially from those He gives authority and a position of responsibility. Those who misuse their authority will have to give an account to the Master. Those who abuse the power given to them and treat their fellow brothers and sisters cruelly because the Lord delays in returning, will face the wrath of the Lord when he returns. But those who are sensible and faithful in their responsibility will be rewarded. (Matthew 24:45-51)

2. VALUE THE RELATIONSHIP THAT WE HAVE WITH GOD

In the parable of the ten virgins in (Matthew 25:1-12) we come across five virgins who value the relationship they have with the bridegroom. In every culture especially the Middle Eastern region, the wedding day is the most important day in the life of a girl. There is much preparation that goes into it and the girls and their families go through a lot of excitement as well as anticipation.

But the other five virgins did not understand, and were unprepared for the arrival of the bridegroom. They did not take oil with them and were left behind because they were not ready. Through this parable, Jesus cautions the Church which is His bride to be ready and to look forward to His coming.

3. BE A GOOD STEWARD OF THE TALENTS GIVEN BY GOD

MATTHEW 25:14-15

"For it is just like a man about to go on a journey, who called his own slaves and entrusted his possessions to them. To one he gave five talents, to another, two, and to another, one, each according to his own ability; and he went on his journey.

In the parable of the Talents in Matthew 25, the Lord revealed that He has given talents to each of us and expects us to be diligent and faithful in handling them. Being good stewards of the gifts and talents God has given us will bring much reward.

God will reward each one according to their faithfulness in using the talents given by Him. The exciting reality is that Jesus will rule over the earth for a thousand years, in a golden period called the Millennium.The Bible declares that we are the heirs of God and co- heirs with Christ. The Bible encourages us not to lose hope when we suffer for the sake of the kingdom of God. This life is a preparation for the life to come.

HEBREWS 10:23–25

Let us hold fast the confession of our hope without wavering, for He who promised is faithful. And let us consider how to stir up one another to love and good works, not neglecting to meet together, as is the habit of some, but encouraging one another, and all the more as you see the Day drawing near……